MEETING LIFE'S CHALLENGES

THE CHRISTIAN READER BOOK ON MEETING LIFE'S CHALLENGES

Edited by Ted Miller

1817

HARPER & ROW, PUBLISHERS, SAN FRANCISCO
Cambridge, Hagerstown, New York, Philadelphia
London, Mexico City, São Paulo, Sydney

FIRST EDITION

Library of Congress Cataloging in Publication Data

Main entry under title:

THE CHRISTIAN READER BOOK ON MEETING LIFE'S CHALLENGES.

1. Christian life—1960– —Addresses, essays, lectures. I. Miller, Ted. II. Christian reader. III. Title: Meeting life's challenges.
BV4501.2.C515   1983   248.4   82-48424
ISBN 0-06-061388-2

---

83 84 85 86 87 10 9 8 7 6 5 4 3 2 1

COPYRIGHT ACKNOWLEDGMENTS

Contents

Challenge of the
80's by Billy Graham

On almost every front—political, economic, social, ecological—our world seems close to the breaking point. Think, for instance, of the chaos that would come to the industrial nations if the flow of oil were cut off! The list of potential disasters lurking around the corner of the 1980s is almost endless. George Orwell's *1984* seems frighteningly close.

Yet for Christians this issue is only part of a greater question: Will we, as Christians, be up to the challenges of the 1980s—whatever they may be? If our sovereign Lord allows us another decade before Christ comes again, will we be able to look back in ten years and say honestly that we have been "good and faithful servants"? As the Apostle Peter says, speaking of the transitory nature of this world and the imminent second coming of Christ, "In view of the fact that all these things are to be dissolved, what sort of people ought you to be?" (2 Pet. 3:11, *Phillips*).

No one has ever found it easy to be a true disciple of Christ; every age poses its temptations to divert us from the path of faithfulness. Sometimes these burst upon us blatantly; sometimes they slip up subtly. The Christian appreciates this if he reads his Bible because "our struggle is not against flesh and blood, but against the rulers, against the authorities, against the powers of this dark world and against the spiritual forces of evil in the heavenly realms" (Eph. 6:12, *NIV*).

The Christian also knows, both from the Bible and church history, that Satan's assaults take different forms in different generations. And he knows the church's opportunities differ in different times. So Christians today must ask what specific challenges and opportunities await us as we face a new decade.

We would be presumptuous to act as if we knew in detail what the world will be like. Nevertheless, we can suggest broad outlines by projecting into the future some of today's significant trends.

1. Great problems will continue to afflict the world. The growing interdependence of nations means that problems once affecting only a few are now affecting virtually everyone on the planet. A domino effect has set in, so that a revolution in Iran or a crop failure in the American Midwest now has serious worldwide repercussions.

These problems will inevitably affect the church. Take, for example, the worldwide economic situation. Few economists believe inflation will disappear soon, and some suggest it will become a permanent fixture on the world scene. No church can build a new building without considering this. No mission board can make long-range plans without allowing for it. No parachurch organization or Christian school can undertake massive expansion without thinking carefully about world economic problems. Many groups are already feeling the pinch, and some may even go out of existence in the 1980s through indifference to economic conditions. The temptation may well beset us to resort to unspiritual gimmicks and unscriptural methods of raising money.

2. The decade will see staggering scientific and technological change. We hear of advances in such areas as medicine and electronics almost every day, and we can expect that trend to continue. Whether countries will always utilize such advances for beneficial purposes is, of course, a different question. And we may wonder whether scientists can solve some of the critical problems we face; but the advance of exotic new discoveries and inventions will surely continue into the 1980s.

Again, evangelicals must be alert to developments that affect our work in the world. Recently I helped dedicate the new facilities of a Christian broadcasting network. I was amazed at the sophisticated equipment, some of the finest in the broadcasting industry. While we must not be dazzled by technology, we must be ready to use every means God gives us to proclaim the gospel. We must also be aware of the ethical issues that accompany the application of certain scientific discoveries, and be ready to give moral guidance to a world that easily succumbs to the manipulation of the many by the few, sometimes in the name of progress.

3. We should remember that a large part of our world continues to drift

10

toward secularism. Large sections of Europe have become virtually secular in outlook, with empty cathedrals standing as monuments to a faith almost completely relegated to the past. In our own nation we see encouraging signs of revival, with countless people coming to faith in Christ; at the same time, secular humanism is still the dominant philosophy. Wheat and tares are growing, almost flourishing, side by side.

The secular mentality is not always openly hostile to religion; it simply leaves God out of life. Our national institutions—education, for example—often exhibit a strong bias against Christian convictions. Charitable deductions and tax exemption for religious organizations will probably continue under fire in the 1980s because of the prevailing secular mentality. Along different lines, the moral decline accompanying our secular trend shows few signs of leveling off. Tolerance toward such patterns of behavior as homosexuality, unmarried couples living together, casual drug use, and numerous other social customs will probably grow. I am convinced that such behavior wreaks inevitable havoc in the personalities of many. Will Christians be prepared to minister compassionately to those who have bought the lie of secular promises and reaped the bitter fruit of such experiences?

4. *The massive resurgence of militant religions moves directly counter to the secularizing trend.* I suspect that such movements are only vaguely comprehended in the West, but they are one of the most important facts of our time. I disagree with those who suggest that this represents a desperate but futile attempt by dying faiths to grasp new life. Militant religions are on the march, and may well become aggressively evangelistic in this decade. I can only imagine what the use of petrodollars to support religious movements might accomplish. Christian missions in the 1980s must cope strategically with resurgent non-Christian religions.

The 1980s therefore may also see an upsurge in religious persecution of Christians. This will not come from militant non-Christian religions alone. As has been true often in church history, secular states can also be savagely anti-Christian. No nation, including our own, can ever assume it is immune from the persecution of true believers—even by the state.

5. *The world of the 1980s will offer vast opportunity for Christians.* As

11

long as we are on this earth, God gives us opportunities to serve him. But I believe the 1980s could be a time of special harvest, one of the greatest in the history of the church, if we rise to the challenge.

We could easily concentrate on the problems. But we must ask: What has the chaotic condition of the world done to people today? We can summarize the answer in one sentence: It has brought countless people to the end of their spiritual rope. Many have run out of answers, and are desperately casting about for something that will bring inner peace, stability, and assurance. I see an unprecedented spiritual hunger today, a restlessness of spirit that can only be satisfied in Jesus.

To evangelical Christians, today's spiritual vacuum should be the greatest fact of our time. Having tried everything except Christ, modern men and women will yield either to despair or to Christ. As with Paul, God is sending us "to open their eyes and turn them from darkness to light, and from the power of Satan to God, so that they may receive forgiveness of sins and a place among those who are sanctified by faith in me" (Acts 26:18).

Surely the 1980s will pose problems. But for the Christian there is no more exciting time to be alive! God is at work in our world, calling men and women in every nation to follow him. And he would remind us how glorious is our calling to be disciples.

Donald Grey Barnhouse was once asked what he would do if he knew Christ was returning tomorrow. He replied that he would do what he had planned. He knew he was doing God's will, and that was all that mattered. Whatever the 1980s hold for us, God calls us to be one thing: faithful. We must commit all that we are to him at the beginning of this new decade, with confidence in the One who said, "Surely I will be with you always, to the very end of the age."

●

God Never Lets Things Just Happen by Paul Little

Have you ever been knocked down by the waves at the seashore? You realize you're in trouble, and you flail around, gasping for breath.

Sometimes life is like that. Tragedy may come; illness may strike; a relationship may fall apart; our financial resources may melt away.

You may not be in such a situation now, but the time will come when the surf of life will knock you down. And then you will want to know how to regain your footing and your spiritual breath.

How can you? The only sure footing in life issues from God. Our confidence in the providential sovereignty of God will anchor our hearts to the fact that our Creator has a loving purpose for each one of us. Nothing happens in your life and mine by accident.

This theme runs through the whole of Scripture from Genesis to Revelation.

Joseph knew it well. He was literally sold down the river by his brothers. In Egypt he was imprisoned because he stood for righteousness. He had every reason for bitterness and hostility, but he was able to say, "You meant it to me for evil, but God meant it to me for good" (Gen. 50:20).

We find the same conviction in Daniel and his three friends, Shadrach, Meshach, and Abednego. King Nebuchadnezzar put it to them clearly: either they must worship his image or be thrown into the fiery furnace. In substance, their answer was, "Look, we don't know what God's plan is, but we believe in his providential sovereignty" (cf. Dan. 3:17, 18).

Then there was David whose life hung by a thread for years because King Saul was out to kill him. And David had a lot of friends who wanted to help God out. They said to David, "Look, there's Saul. We'll take care of him for you. The blood won't even be on your hands."

But David, knowing God's providence and love, answered, "The Lord forbid that I should stretch out my hand against the Lord's anointed" (1 Sam. 26:11 NASB).

These and other great men of the Bible knew about the providential sovereignty of God. Of course, they knew him first as the Lord of their lives, their deliverer from sin through confession and faith. That relationship is essential.

Let's see how God's sovereignty operated in the life of the Apostle Paul. We can see it in the opening chapter of Paul's letter to the Philippians.

In Philippians 1 Paul is not writing from the local Holiday Inn; he is a Roman prisoner. Yet even in those circumstances he was able to see the providential, loving sovereignty of God operating in his past, his present, and his future.

The whole situation had begun in Jerusalem (Acts 21:27–40). He had been sent to jail on what we would call a "bum rap" today. He had been wrongly accused of taking a Gentile into the temple, because the Jews had seen Trophimus the Ephesian with him. In the uproar that resulted he was put into what we call protective custody.

Ultimately, you recall, Paul appealed to Caesar. He was brought to Rome, where he wrote the Philippian letter. Here he was a prisoner, at first no doubt in a Roman prison. Later he lived in his own lodgings, chained to Roman soldiers on a rotating basis, while awaiting trial under the corrupt, unstable emperor, Nero.

It is in that context that Paul wrote that amazing statement, "Now I want you to know, brethren, that my circumstances have turned out for the greater progress of the gospel" (Phil. 1:12 NASB).

Paul saw the hand of God in his past circumstances. He knew that nothing had happened to him by accident, that God had been working out his purposes. It was this awareness of God's purposeful goodness that kept Paul from being overwhelmed in the surf of life.

Have you recognized that fact about your past? Every one of us has things in his past he wonders about, things he wishes had been different, but it is God who has brought us through. We need to recognize that fact.

God has allowed the struggles which have come into your life, be they relational, financial, or physical. He has allowed stresses. He has been at work in them for your good.

14

Have you ever thanked him for his providential, sovereign, and loving care up to the present? Have you been thankful, or have you indulged in second guessing? Maybe you have said, "If only I had said this, or done that, or somebody hadn't done this or that, the whole thing might have been different."

Do you wish you were somebody else or that you were doing something else? You may find yourself fighting God if you fail to realize, as Paul did here, that God has had his hand in all your past.

This may include failures on your part. Though you may have fallen short at certain points, God is most concerned with the present and your relationship to him from this place on. Whatever may have happened, you didn't take God by surprise. He loves you and he purposes good in all his providential, sovereign working.

However, we need to see that accepting God's providential sovereignty does not mean we should be passive. It does not mean acceptance of what Muslims call *Kismet*, the blind out-working of fate.

It does not mean that we lack freedom of choice or responsibility. We are to be active where activity is required, but we are to accept that which we cannot control as coming through the hand of God.

When Paul had been falsely accused and thrown in prison in Philippi, he and Silas had sung at midnight. As a result the jailer had been converted and his family with him.

But later, when the magistrates had discovered he was a Roman citizen and wanted him to slip away quietly, Paul had refused. "Nothing doing," he had said in effect. "You violated my rights as a Roman citizen. Come down here personally, get us out of jail and escort us out of town" (Acts 16:37–39).

Paul had accepted the fact that he was in jail, and because of his experience somebody was converted. But later he had made a scene for the glory of God. He had wanted to make it clear to them and to the whole Roman Empire that it was not against the law to preach the gospel.

Paul acted when he could to change the situation; but when he couldn't change things, he accepted them. We should do the same.

Can you recognize the providential sovereignty of God in your present situation? Maybe you are going through something that really troubles you. You do not understand; you don't see how it fits together.

Take courage. Ask God to show you what he is doing. Maybe there are dimensions of blessing that you have overlooked. If you can't see them clearly, realize in the light of the Word of God that he is working in your present circumstances.

Why was Paul used of God even in prison? First, Paul wasn't wallowing in self-pity. He wasn't saying, "Why me?" Paul took his circumstances as from God and made the best of them.

Second, Paul didn't think God had forgotten him. In fact, he took his current situation as an appointment from God. In verse 16 he says, "Knowing that I am appointed for the defense of the gospel."

Do you see what Paul is saying? He is saying, "They know [and they must have gotten it from him] that all these things are part of God's design."

Do you feel God has forgotten you? Remind yourself, as our Lord says in Matthew 10:30, "The very hairs of your head are all numbered." He knows all about that decision or problem or difficulty, and he hasn't made a mistake. He has set you in your situation for a special purpose.

The third reason Paul was used of God was that he lived in the "now." In verse 20 he says it is his hope and earnest expectation that "Christ shall even now, as always, be exalted in my body, whether by life or by death."

Paul could have said, "Well, Lord, I guess this part of my experience is an interlude in my ministry and I can coast." But he didn't. He realized that God's will is not some package in the future, let down from heaven on a string, but a scroll that unrolls each day.

He knew that God had a will and plan and purpose for him today and again tomorrow and the next day. And God has a plan like that for you. The only day you and I have for sure to live for Jesus Christ is now—today.

The Christian life is not some great, successful exploit out in the future. It is an accumulation of days of living for Jesus Christ. Only what you and I put into today will determine the quality and content of our total Christian lives.

Paul also saw the providential sovereignty of God in his future. Circumstances were uncertain; Nero was totally unpredictable. The apostle did not know what the outcome was going to be, but he knew that "this shall turn out for my deliverance" (1:19).

At that point he wasn't talking about being freed from jail, but about his good. Then he says he is in a great tension, desiring that "Christ shall even now, as always, be exalted in my body, whether by life or by death."

Paul wasn't looking to death as a cop-out, but rather as the fulfillment of the ministry God had given him. He had confidence in God for the future, whatever it might be.

Your future and mine are uncertain, too. But if we have seen the providential sovereignty of God in our past and if we are aware of his presence and power in the immediate present, then we can relax about the way ahead.

Never has there been more uncertainty in the world. There are no entirely safe places, politically, physically, economically. Yet our lives are in God's hands if we belong to him, and we can trust him to unfold the future as we are active in working out his purposes.

Nothing happens by accident. And we can rest with confidence in that. ●

The Girl Who Likes Adventure by Kay Oliver

Becki Conway is homecoming queen of Urbana (IL) High School. She's been a cheerleader, and on the track team. Her life whirls around school, working at Wendy's, Campus Life activities, youth group activities at Twin City Bible Church, and lots of time with lots of friends.

A versatile athlete, she plays volleyball and soccer, rides bikes and horses, roller skates, swims, dives, skis—all on one leg. Her left leg, amputated a year ago, has been replaced by a prosthesis.

"This is Harold the Hairless Wonder," Becki volunteers. "Wanta see how he works?"

Before a visitor has a chance to wonder how to mention the unmentionable, Becki has put everyone at ease, demonstrating Harold's flexible knee and showing how he's attached and how he works.

Rather than seeing Harold as a hindrance, Becki is sure it's in God's special plan.

Becki first noticed problems with her knee during eighth grade cheerleading. "The tendons are being strained during a fast growth period," a doctor diagnosed. "She'll outgrow it." But the problem persisted.

A biopsy in the fall of 1976 revealed a benign growth localized within the bone wall. Puzzled, the doctors kept watch.

A second biopsy in the fall of 1977 revealed a growing tumor. Local doctors planned removal of the tumor and a bone graft. But just to be sure, they sent a sample of the biopsy to many labs, including one where, as Becki explains it, the "great grandaddy of weird tumors" took a look.

Becki got her first clue that things could be serious when her doctor, who attends their church, called on a Tuesday night to see

whether her parents, Jim and Sally Conway, would be at the church dinner that night. What an obvious question—Jim is pastor.

"I was pretty sure something was wrong," Becki says. "Maybe just a woman's intuition. Because I had homework, I wasn't going to the dinner. So I had some time to prepare myself. I watered my plants, baked some brownies, and thought.

"I knew God could heal my leg. But I also knew that he would do what would benefit me the most, and what would benefit the people around me.

"And, morbid as it might sound, I had a tingle of excitement. I knew something big was coming. And I like an adventure."

When her parents came home, Becki knew the news was sad. "When the door opened," Becki says, "a big cloud of heaviness moved in. I could just feel it. My parents were quiet. My mom's eyes were red. And the doctor was with them."

They sat together in the living room as the doctor explained in detail the medical board's decision. They would have to amputate. "Becki," he said tenderly, "for two weeks I've been racking my mind. But there just is no better way."

Stunned, Becki didn't feel like crying. "I could see my parents were in the pits," she explains, "so I knew I couldn't get depressed. They needed my support."

The news came just before spring break. The family had planned a week's vacation in Florida with Becki's sisters Brenda and Barbara, both students at Taylor University, and with family friends. The doctor agreed the surgery could wait. One caution: no sunburns allowed.

During that week the family strengthened their ties and their love. They talked openly about the amputation and prayed. Jim Conway was especially convinced that "whatever ye shall ask in prayer, believing, ye shall receive." And he was asking God for healing.

While running on the beach, Becki occasionally wondered what life would be like with an artificial leg. She enjoyed shocking people by saying, "See this leg? I'm getting it cut off!" But most of the time, she says, "God just didn't let me dwell on it. I wasn't blocking it out of my mind. That would have been the cheater's way out. God just helped me to accept that it was going to happen."

The night before surgery, Becki experienced real peace. She wondered about practical things—such as taking showers. And joked about having one less leg to shave. But her concern was to serve and please God.

"I knew God would work through me," she says. "But I wasn't sure I would be what he wanted me to be. I didn't want to fail him."

Pain from the amputation was excruciating. Then came the phantom pains, when the convalescent felt pain where the leg used to be. Her short stump was swollen to the size of a basketball. Friends were afraid to come in—afraid of what they'd see, afraid of what to say.

Becki took charge. "Wanta see my basketball?" she'd ask. Or, "Come on in and see stumpy!" Her openness helped to conquer their fears, and she soon had a steady stream of visitors.

To her parents' and doctors' amazement, Becki never felt bitterness or depression. She really accepted reality.

How?

"I knew my God," Becki says confidently. "I had been saved as a child, and had given God my life. He was my friend, and I knew he wasn't going to let this experience be wasted.

"Besides, my leg is small compared to the rest of me. My strength comes from the inside. God will one day give me a new leg. Until then, it's just like the Bible says. These old bodies of ours make us groan. They are a pain, a bother. That's especially true for me. But in heaven I'll have a glorified body. I'll have Harold the rest of my life. But that's such a short time, compared to eternity."

Ten days after the amputation she went to a track meet on crutches. Friends who knew how much running meant to her were amazed. Becki explained her source of strength.

"They always knew I was a pastor's kid, and that I was religious," Becki says. "But a lot of people fit that category. Now they could see that God is really active in my life."

Becki says her missing leg creates a deeper dependency on God—a built-in humblizer, she calls it.

"Whenever I start to pull away from God—even a little bit—and feel sorry for myself, I start to go down. That happened once, and it made me realize how much I really depend on God and on the Scriptures. Whenever I start serving myself, then I'm no longer fully serving God. And I can't be happy."

If Becki's response to tragedy seems surprisingly positive, her father's response was surprisingly negative.

Jim Conway, who had been preaching and giving God's comfort to others for 25 years, found the trial almost unbearable.

"I was certain God would heal Becki," he says quietly. "God tells us again and again to pray and we will receive. This was not wishful thinking on my part. God said to pray in faith, and I was obeying."

So strongly did Jim believe, that the day of surgery he made the doctor promise to test Becki's leg again before amputating.

"A crowd of friends from the church had come to wait with us. So many came in, in fact, that they made us leave the waiting room. When the surgeon came out, I knew what he was going to say, and I couldn't face it. I couldn't face all those people. So I ran.

"I ran to the hospital basement where no one would find me. And I cried. I yelled. I pounded my fists against the wall. I felt like the God whom I had served had abandoned me at the hour of my deepest need. Was he so busy answering prayers for parking places that he couldn't see Becki?

"Either God had the power to heal Becki and had refused—in that case, he was cruel—or he really couldn't heal as he promised. The Scriptures now seemed like a hoax. So how could I trust any of the rest of it?"

As Jim poured out his anguish, two friends—another pastor and the Youth for Christ director—found him. They listened patiently. Neither tried to answer his emotional accusations against God, nor did they berate him. Instead they accepted his anguish and loved him.

Jim knew that without confidence in Scripture, he could not minister. That Sunday a visiting Glee Club was scheduled, so he did not have to preach. The following Wednesday, however, he was scheduled to speak at Taylor University.

Students had been praying for Becki. So Jim told them what had happened, and that he had many questions. He admitted his faltering faith, then emphasized that they should be forming friendships, for only his closest friends had been able to help.

"I knew he was still God's man with God's message," his wife Sally confides. "I never doubted that God would help him work through this and once again use him."

Many well-meaning people tried to give "answers" for why God had allowed such suffering. Some said he preached too much on the love of God and should preach more on justice. Others suggested hidden sin. Or that he needed more faith. One said perhaps God allowed this to bring the church closer together.

"Well," Jim answered, "if it's like everything else, this church unity will last about six months. Then what will God do? Take her other leg? An arm? There's not enough of Becki to keep the church revived."

Jim, who has a master's in counseling, understands that people can't handle situations that have no obvious answer. So they manufacture answers.

That Sunday he preached a message similar to the one at Taylor. By this time he could say that "as irrational as it seems, God knows what he's doing. Even though I have no answers, I know that God is alive and is doing what he knows to be best."

Jim then left for a two-week seminar in California. There he spent intense time with six other pastors who ministered deeply to him. By the end of the two weeks, he saw a new dimension:

"I became aware in a new way that when Christ was on the cross, the Father could have delivered him but he did not. I accepted the fact that God could have healed Becki, but he deliberately chose not to.

He knew that I was going to be angry, and he was willing to put up with me. He has a higher purpose. I still don't know what that purpose is, but I have a new grip on the situation. I no longer *have* to have an answer. I must let God be God."

It still hurt Jim and Sally to see their daughter hop on one leg, but her ability to cope helped their healing process. At one point Sally said to Becki, "Honey, I know you have good balance and can hop. But it's tearing Daddy up to see you. Please, for his sake, use your crutches."

"Mom," Becki answered, "if Dad's having problems, that's because he isn't accepting me as I am. This is *me*. I have only one leg. And Dad needs to accept it. No, I won't use the crutches."

With time Jim and Sally came to see that although God had not given miraculous physical healing, he had healed emotionally.

"Becki has an unusually mature perspective on life and death and on the body," Jim explains, fatherly pride lighting his face. "She has settled the issue, and sees that physical perfection and length of life are irrelevant. The loss of her leg has given her real freedom. She isn't a slave to her body. Her body is a servant to her."

And a servant to God, may I add. ●

When God Does Not Answer by Gordon Chilvers

A godly farmer I once knew faced bankruptcy. Local competitors had acted unfairly and he had not been able to sell his produce at the best prices. He needed $4,000 promptly to pay his creditors. One wealthy man owed him $5,000. He asked God to urge the man to send his check promptly.

The creditors pressed harder. The farmer prayed more urgently for his $5,000, but received no answer. He was puzzled. He had always given generously, attended church regularly, helped neighbors in difficulty. Why should God not help him in his distress?

No check came and the creditors demanded payment. Finally he set a day on which he would sell his stock and implements. The day for the auction arrived, with still no check in the mail. Heavy-hearted, he left the house and went a few miles away so he would not have to see his cherished farm sold before his eyes. God had not answered his prayer. Why?

We are sure that God can answer any petition more rapidly than any computer can answer our question. Indeed he has a start on any computer. He says: "Before they call, I will answer; and while they are yet speaking, I will hear" (Isa. 65:24).

Peter cried out to the Lord as he was drowning, and Jesus grasped his hand immediately. The dying thief asked Jesus to remember him, and Jesus answered him promptly. Yet Abraham longed for the son God had promised and after 20 years Isaac was still not born.

Martha and Mary sent word to Jesus that their brother Lazarus was seriously ill. But Jesus did not start out at once. He stayed beyond Jordan two more days, just long enough for Lazarus to die. No, even in those early times our Lord's answer to prayer was not always immediate.

25

When we see no immediate answer to our prayer, we should first examine our lives to see if there are any hindrances. These include the presence of willful sin (Ps. 66:18), unbelief (James 1:6, 7), praying out of the will of God (1 John 5:14, 15), disobedience (1 John 3:21, 22), selfishness (James 4:3), an unforgiving spirit (Matt. 6:14), and meanness (Prov. 21:13). When none of these hindrances seems to apply, why does God still delay answers to our prayers?

Does a delay mean God has no intention of answering? Or is it possible that while our request may be good, our idea of when we ought to have it is wrong?

However urgently they implore us, we do not give four-year-old Dorothy a box of matches for her experiments, five-year-old James a razor-sharp knife for a toy, or six-year-old Donald a solid gold watch. Matches, sharp knives, and gold watches have excellent uses, yet we cannot answer promptly when we know a delay will be better for our children.

Eleanor Wagner, a missionary working in Africa, was seriously ill with a stomach disease while living far from medical help. She longed for good food, but had spent all her money. The missionary implored God for her monthly check to arrive at once. Nothing came. For thirty days she endured a monotonous diet of almost tasteless oatmeal and canned milk. At last the check came.

Home on furlough, she related her experience at a public meeting. Afterward a doctor asked her the nature of her illness. She described to him her digestive malfunction. "The delayed check saved your life," exclaimed the doctor. "Thirty days of oatmeal diet is the best treatment for your disease."

Delay in answers to our prayer can bring advantages we would not otherwise realize. A faith that survives delay becomes purer and stronger. Delay can strengthen our spiritual lives and make us more mature Christians.

A Christian man was serving with the American forces in Europe. Two months earlier Germany had collapsed with the suicide of Hitler. The man was praying to get back home quickly, eager to rejoin his lonely wife and to see his son, who had been born just after he had left America.

Suddenly the man learned he had been assigned to Japan for an indefinite period. He was stunned.

Fifteen years later, then a mature Christian known for his Christlike character, the man said in retrospect, "That delay shook my faith to its foundations. Yet during that year in Japan I learned more of God and his love for me than I had learned in any period of my life. That year is when I began to trust God completely."

By the time of Isaac's birth, Abraham had learned to trust God for everything. He was even prepared to sacrifice Isaac, believing that God could raise him from the dead, though the world had never seen a resurrection. By the time Samuel was born, Hannah's devotion to the Lord had deepened enormously and she willingly dedicated him to life-long service in the temple.

A delay may also be a pointer that God's solution to our problem is better than our own.

When the disappointed farmer I mentioned earlier went back home, expecting to see his yard empty, he found the stock and implements still there. Had nobody bought it? Yes, the neighbors had paid a fair price for it all; then had given everything back to him so he could start again!

True, the farmer did not get his check when he had expected it. It arrived one week later, giving him ample working capital. God had moved a different group of people to extricate him from the crisis!

Sometimes the delay to prayer is so long that an answer, if it does come, seems too late. We cannot be sure that we shall always know why God has not answered. Yet we may still rest in the knowledge that God is too wise to err.

Sometimes God delays his answer to give us something better than we had asked. William Gurnall, the seventeenth century English Puritan, wrote: "Some prayers have a longer voyage than others, but they return with the richer lading at last, so that the praying soul is a gainer by waiting for an answer."

That outstanding man of prayer George Mueller testified: "I have myself had to wait a long time to get certain blessings. In many instances the answer has come instantaneously. In other things I had to wait ten years, fifteen, twenty years and upward; yet invariably at the last the answer has come."

When delay occurs in our receiving answers to our prayers, we need not necessarily conclude that God has said no. He rewards all who seek him diligently. ●

I Was a Social Drinker by Fred H. Baker

I am one of almost 10 million Americans who "knew I would never have a drinking problem."

Now that I have walked into the dark tunnel, with the walls crashing in behind me and no light ahead, I am compelled to tell what alcoholism means.

My compulsion comes naturally: I have lost the choice between drinking or abstinence. Although I am now well along into my fourth year without a drink, I will always be an alcoholic; anybody who doesn't understand that I cannot be "cured" doesn't know even the ABC's of alcoholism. If you don't realize that my using your brand of mouthwash could mean I would die a drunk, all I can ask is that you learn a little more about booze before repeating folk tales.

My qualifications to write are admittedly limited. The more I know about alcoholism the more I realize, to use the words of Alcoholics Anonymous, alcohol is cunning, baffling, and powerful. As executive director of one of the nation's larger recovery homes for alcoholics, with almost 70 men in residence at all times, I have had a lot of exposure, which has only humbled me.

My experiences convince me that the unprinted news behind much of the bad news in our newspapers is too devastating—and personal—to print. The highway fatality, the sex-triangle quarrel and murder, many in the long list of divorces, and the suicide had one thing in common—booze.

Even in evangelical churches and, yes, even in churches requiring total abstinence, America's Number 1 drug—alcohol—is *the problem* behind so many problems. When hidden or denied, it erupts so violently, like a volcano that gives out only a few rumbling hints of trouble.

Within the last few years a prominent, Bible-quoting congressman died of "natural causes" after a long succession of hospitalizations. Those of us who know first-hand what alcohol can do would describe it differently.

"Naturally," we would say, "he finally died." Most of his constituents supported him to the end; such a Bible-quoter could not possibly be an alcoholic. But 19 of 20 alcoholics die as they live—as drinking alcoholics.

Alcoholism is an old story; if he had chosen to do so, the tippling congressman could have read it in the last verses of Proverbs 23. The paraphrase in *The Living Bible* says in part, ". . . You will stagger like a sailor tossed at sea, clinging to a swaying mast. And afterwards you will say, 'I didn't know it when they beat me up . . . . Let's go and have another drink!' "

It took becoming an alcoholic for me to see what the Bible has to say about the "other side" of drinking, even though in biblical days only a mild wine and a crude "beer" were available.

Back in the days when I drank "responsibly," as I liked to term it, I knew all about Paul telling Timothy to take a little wine for his tummy, and how the Greek word definitely meant wine and that therefore Christ himself likely indulged. So, why shouldn't I? Now I know. In 1970 I found out how amazing God's grace really is; like many others who have come to Phoenix from throughout the United States and Canada, I discovered that "Amazing Grace" was far more than a black disc in the top 40 tunes of the day. Thank God, alcoholics can and do recover. Unbelievably I am sober, not dead, today.

I cannot fault Christ's Church for doing so little to help the alcoholic. We alcoholics do everything we can to hide and deny our problem until, humanly speaking, we are beyond any hope of recovery. We cry out in desperation, "Nobody understands, not even God!" I had been very active in the church; there are those who said God used me in those days to lead them to a saving knowledge of Christ as their Lord and Savior. Yet, in my crisis, it appeared that my God had condemned and forsaken me. Distorted thinking? Of course. Befuddled, alcoholic thinking. But how many in the church do understand? Very few, too few.

Facts should disturb some of the complacency.

Last year the per capita consumption of alcoholic beverages in America was 26 gallons. Stop, think! Convert that number into weeks—a half gallon a week for every man, woman, and child! Beer, wine, gin, vodka, whiskey, and the rest.

Subtract the kids and the total abstainers, and the lowest figure I can come up with as to the number of those who do drink is close to 110 million. That almost doubles the figure to a gallon a week!

Estimates vary, but it seems reasonable that about one-fourth of those who drink consume three-fourths of the total, or three gallons in a week. Is it any wonder that the U.S. Department of Transportation estimates that one of every 10 drivers is an alcoholic? Isn't it reasonable to assume that many more are well on the way into a problem?

I must submit that the rest of America has a problem, too. It cannot understand. It is easy to dismiss problem drinking and alcoholism as "just a sin," but the problem goes on. There is the old-fashioned appeal to willpower; as an alcoholic, I must ask, "What willpower?" I had it, except when it came to booze; there it was gone.

"Why not just stop?" asks the one who has little knowledge of the problem. In a very dramatic way, many alcoholics do just that. Our suicide rate is 40 times the national average, and we're included in the average. Twice I had come to think that was the only way I could stop. Insane? Yes and no. To continue is to "feel no pain," until a friendly doctor lists a "natural" cause of death to spare the hurt of family, friends, and the church. To stop is to suffer beyond belief. To resume is such sweet relief.

Actually, any suggestion that the problem drinker "can stop any time he or she wants to" is an insidious invitation to continue drinking. Alcoholics do not seek help until that point is long past. A Christian friend of mine, now with 27 years of sobriety, put it this way, his memory still vivid: "Nobody feels the pain when falling; it's the stopping that hurts so bad."

Perhaps the biggest problem, however, is with the individual—and the church has many of them—who says, "It won't happen to me." We all said that.

I remember well the young mother, a total abstainer until her mid-20's. It was that time of the month and she had to work all day at her church; she couldn't face it. A friend recommended Geritol, or Nyquil, or a little terpin hydrate as a tonic; none was on hand, but the magic ingredient in each was the same as in a bottle of vodka. Purely as a "tonic," really medicinal, she had her "first drink." In six months she was up to more than a quart of vodka a day; not typical, but possible.

When I entered Calvary Rehabilitation Center in Phoenix, I was 47, well under the average admittance age of 55; today I am 51, six years older than the "average" resident. But those teenagers a visitor might see at Calvary aren't there to visit dad. They, too, can no longer live with or without alcohol.

To you who are nondrinkers, please understand how difficult it is to understand, and that you probably do not. Please do not warn the alcoholic man or woman about going to hell in a hurry; for someone who "knows it's impossible to stop" may feel that God might show a little mercy if a person stopped—violently. Too many whom I have known and loved are dead; too many of those still living and hurting are running away or rebelling against that God. Please let those talk who know that God's love can and does extend to the alcoholic.

If you do drink "temperately," I know I can't argue you into the abstinence that is a choice of life or death for me. From my own experience, if you ever "need" a drink—to celebrate, to grieve, to relax, to sleep, to pass that time of month or just to escape a day's frustrations, you're on your way. The blinkers are on, the train is coming fast; will you beat it? I did not.

There was a time when I could say, "There but for the grace of God go I." Now I have to say, "There I went!" My sin was pride; I was the master of my fate; it would never happen to me, but it did. In my complete defeat, concerned Christians who "understood" held out their hands and God gave me the impossible: victory, as of today. My pride is still too great for complacency; I must turn every day back to God for the grace I need, but that's a wonderful way to live. ●

Joy in a Wheelchair by Philip Yancey and Joni Eareckson

*Y*ou reach Joni Eareckson's home by winding through the abrupt hills west of Baltimore, following the river. You are surrounded by hardwood forest until you reach the crest of the highest hill, where a sweeping panoramic landscape suddenly unfolds. Joni's house is on such a hill. It's a cottage made of large boulders and hand-hewn timber, painstakingly fitted together by her father. Joni's studio juts out over the hill, its glass walls allowing a perfect view. A brown stallion is grazing in the valley, swishing his tail at flies. A Great Dane is romping through the grass.

Many artists live tucked away in rustic settings like this one. But Joni's life is different from the others. She never leaves her studio without someone pushing her. And she draws with her mouth. She has to—she's paralyzed—her hands are limp and useless.

In high school, blonde, good-looking Joni was voted "outstanding girl athlete" by her classmates. She captained the basketball team, played on the lacrosse team, and excelled in horse shows.

Now, Joni's daily exercise consists of slight movements. She can move her arm with biceps and shoulder motion. So, by hooking a fork into a metal slot on her hand brace, she can feed herself. And by keeping her fingernails long, she can turn the pages of a book. Most of her day is taken up with the process of drawing—meticulous, subtle nods and slides of her head as she bites down on a brush with her teeth. Slowly, a recognizable scene takes form: horses, skiers, youth.

Nine years have passed since the accident, yet Joni's face is alive, her eyes bright and expressive. Her spirit is so effervescent that she brings to mind those "Think positive" Miss Americas. But unlike them, Joni's spirit was squeezed out of tragedy. She tells how everything changed.

"Summer had been especially hot and humid that year, 1967. July was stifling. I practiced with the horses in the morning, working up such a sweat only a dip in the bay could cool me. My sister and I rode to the Chesapeake Bay beach and dove into the murky water.

32

"I was never content to swim laps in a pool or splash around in the shallow part of the bay. I liked free swimming, in the open water. A raft floating 50 or 60 yards offshore was a perfect target, and my sister and I raced to it. We were both athletic, and sometimes reckless.

"When I reached the raft, I climbed on it and quickly dove off the side. It was a fast motion, done almost without thinking. I felt the pull of the water . . . and then a stunning jar—my head crashed into a rock on the bottom. I couldn't move. It was awful. With my mind I was telling my muscles to swim, but nothing was happening. I held my breath and waited, suspended facedown in the water.

"My sister, noticing I hadn't surfaced, searched underwater until she found me. She pulled me to the top. I gasped for air. I tried to hold on to her, but again my muscles would not respond. She draped me over her shoulder and began paddling toward shore."

Joni spent the next several months in a hospital bed. The pain was not great, and doctors hoped some of her nerves would repair themselves. Only after several months of medical reports did it sink in that she would not get well. Her whole lifestyle would change. No more sports cars, horse shows, lacrosse matches. Maybe no more dates. She was devastated.

The inevitable questions crept in: Why so cruel a blow at such a prime time in her life? Was God trying to punish her? She became so despondent she begged her best friend to bring pills so she could commit suicide.

Joni had been a regular at church and in Young Life club in high school, but she wasn't interested in the "moment-by-moment spiritual stuff other kids were into." Her turning to God was slow. Change from bitterness and confusion to trust in him dragged out over three years of tears and violent questionings.

One night especially, Joni became convinced that God did understand. Pain was streaking through her back in a way that is a unique torment to the paralyzed. Cindy, one of Joni's closest friends, was beside her bed, searching desperately for some way to cheer Joni. Finally, she clumsily blurted out, "Joni, Jesus knows how you feel—you aren't the only one . . . he was paralyzed too."

Joni stared at her. "What? What are you talking about?"

Cindy continued, "It's true. Remember, he was nailed on the cross. His back was raw from beatings, and he must have yearned for a way to change positions or redistribute his weight. But he couldn't. He was paralyzed by the nails."

The thought had never occurred to her that God had felt the exact piercing sensations that racked her body. The idea was profoundly comforting to Joni.

"God became incredibly close to me. Few of us have the luxury—it took me forever to think of it as that—to come to ground zero with God. Before the accident, my questions had always been, 'How will God fit into this situation? How will he affect my dating life? My career plans? The things I most like to do?' All those options were gone. It was me, just a helpless body, and God. Some of the verses I had learned at Young Life camp would come back to me, like when Jesus promised 'life in all its fullness.' Could that promise still apply to me, when it looked as if all the fullness of life had been taken away?

"I had no other identity but God, and gradually he became enough. I became overwhelmed with the phenomenon of the personal God, who created the universe, living in my life. He would make me attractive and worthwhile—I could not do it without him.

"The first months, even years, I was consumed with the unanswered questions of what God was trying to teach me. I probably secretly hoped that by figuring out God's ideas, I could learn my lesson and then he would heal me.

"I guess every Christian with an experience similar to mine goes back to the book of Job for answers. Here was a man who deserved no punishment, yet he suffered more than I could imagine. Everything was taken away from him. Strangely, the book of Job does not answer any questions about why God let the tragedies happen. Instead, God was interested in Job's response. He wanted Job to tightly, stubbornly cling to him even when it looked as if God were the enemy. Job hung in there, and God rewarded him.

" 'Is that what God wants?' I wondered. My focus changed from demanding an explanation from God to humbly depending on him.

"Okay, I am paralyzed. It's terrible. I don't like it. But can God still use me, paralyzed? Can I, paralyzed, still worship God and love him? He has taught me that I can.

"Maybe God's gift to me is my dependence on him. I will never reach the place where I'm self-sufficient, where God is crowded out of my life. I'm aware of his grace to me every moment. My need for his help is obvious every day when I wake up, flat on my back, waiting for someone to come dress me. I can't even comb my hair or blow my nose alone!

"Somehow—and it took me three years to admit—God proved to me that I, too, can have a fullness of life. I have friends who care. I have the beauty of the outdoors. Though I can't splash in the creek and ride the horses, I can sit outside and my senses are flooded with smells and textures and beautiful sights.

"The peace that counts is an internal peace, and God has lavished that peace on me.

"And there's one more thing. I have hope for the future. The Bible speaks of our bodies being 'glorified' in heaven. In high school that was always a hazy, foreign concept. But now I realize that I will be healed. I haven't been cheated out of being a complete person—I'm just going through a 40-year delay, and God is with me even through that.

"Being 'glorified'—I know the meaning of that now. It's the time, after my death here, when I'll be on my feet dancing!" ●

Praise the Lord — Anyhow? by Harold L. Mitton

Should we give thanks to God in the midst of any adversity and suffering? The woman we were listening to thought we should. She said she had done so and had experienced a great release in spite of a family calamity. Her son had been involved in an automobile accident and had sustained painful injuries. The car itself was a write-off; and yet she was able to praise God.

Some people were greatly helped by the speaker's witness that she was willing to give thanks in such dire circumstances, but others were either offended or downright incredulous. All kinds of questions began to boil in the minds of those present: Was the woman sincere? Was she a fanatic? Had she misunderstood the words of the Apostle Paul to the Christians of Thessalonica: "In everything give thanks"?

I have often reflected upon the heated discussion that took place as a result of this woman's testimony. I confess that her line of reasoning has not always been my reaction to crisis or calamity. This has to be one of the areas of growth in my spiritual life.

When you get down to brass tacks, as my mother used to say, only a few options are available for handling adverse circumstances. We can curse God or curse our luck; we can be angry with the universe; we can indulge in self-pity. Someone has said that humans are especially prone to three temptations: to whine, to shine, and to recline!

If Christians are not to handle life's calamities by giving expression to anger, self-pity, cynicism, or despair, how are we to respond? Perhaps the suggestion that we are to give thanks in every situation is not so bizarre after all. I perhaps should have known this all along: it is the moment of adversity which "separates the men from the boys." Surely, it doesn't require any spiritual grace to rejoice when everything in life is going swimmingly.

Granted all this, I still have some difficulty in knowing how to interpret these words of the apostle: "In everything give thanks." One cannot be thankful that people starve. One cannot be thankful that many people suffer from the scourge of war and disease and economic oppression. And certainly one cannot be thankful when suffering comes to someone else.

What the Apostle Paul is stating here is something deeply personal. He is suggesting that while believers may not be able to give thanks to God for everything that happens, they can give thanks in spite of everything that happens. I do not believe this is simply playing with words.

This much we know: no matter how bleak our circumstances may be, we are not forsaken of God! This, in itself, is cause for rejoicing! How much more credible is our witness before the world if we take adversity on the chin, not in stoical fashion but with praise which is born out of faith in God's unchanging goodness. In fact, this may be faith's most crucial test: our reaction to adverse circumstances.

It is difficult to defeat and dishearten the person who remains serenely thankful. There is something triumphant about praise. Not a few people have told me that the only thing that saved them from the grip of melancholia was the therapy of thanksgiving. It should be a helpful exercise for us to look more closely at the Apostle's ability to be thankful in all circumstances.

The Apostle Paul was grateful to God for the supreme gift of his love in Christ. In writing to the Corinthians he exclaimed, "Thanks be unto God for his unspeakable gift." This had to be the driving force of Paul's life: gratitude for the unspeakable gift of God's salvation through the life, death, and resurrection of his Son, Jesus Christ. Why was Paul willing to endure hardship, persecution, scourging, imprisonment, shipwreck, and even martyrdom? There can be but one answer: gratitude.

A period of great testing comes at one time or another to every faithful Christian. The mood in which I found myself one day was as black as a moonless night. My sense of self-worth had been taking a severe beating when my secretary informed me that a businessman, whose first name was John, wanted to see me. He said he had dropped by because he felt prompted to do so. It seems he had been deeply moved by something I had said on a previous Sunday, and he wanted me to know it. After he left, the words of Scripture kept ringing in my ears: "There was a man sent from God, whose name was John." Like Paul, I thanked God and took courage.

Finally, Paul was grateful to God for victory even in suffering. To the Corinthians he wrote, "Thanks be unto God, which always causeth us to triumph in Christ." What is so unique about the apostle's attitude is that he exhorts his fellow believers to "rejoice always," "on every occasion," "in every set of circumstances." We find in Colossians 1:24 a striking confession of Paul's own rejoicing in the midst of suffering. The apostle both taught and practiced the principle of praying unceasingly and of giving thanks in every circumstance.

One day, we are told, Johann Tauler of Strasbourg met a peasant. "God give you a good day, my friend," he greeted him.

The peasant answered briskly, "I thank God I never have a bad day."

Tauler, astonished, kept silence for a space. Then he added, "God give you a happy life, my friend."

The peasant replied composedly, "I thank God I am never unhappy."

"Never unhappy!" cried Tauler. "What do you mean?"

"Well," came the response, "when it is fine I thank God, when it rains I thank God, when I have plenty I thank God, when I am hungry I thank God; and since God's will is my will, and whatever pleases him pleases me, why should I say that I am unhappy when I am not?"

Tauler looked upon him with awe. "Who are you?" he asked.

"I am a king," said the peasant.

"A king?" Tauler gasped. "Where is your kingdom?"

The peasant smiled gravely. "In my heart," he whispered softly.

I covet this kind of spiritual maturity: "In everything give God thanks." ●

Two Lauras, One Miracle

by Laura Cheney

In a crowded room or the halls at school, I would often hear somebody call "Hey, Laura!" I'd turn around expecting a smile or a wave—but it was always the *other* Laura they were talking to. I'd feel so small and insignificant I'd want to crawl into a deep hole and hide.

How I envied Laura Nash. I'd see her surrounded by friends—laughing and talking—the center of attention wherever she went. Her sparkling dark eyes, shoulder-length blonde hair, and winning smile always made a big hit with the guys. She is everything that I wished to be.

How can a person be accepted by others when she can't accept herself? I was more than 25 pounds overweight—having to look in the mirror was almost more than I could bear. My clothes didn't fit right and I could never wear any of the popular styles. I couldn't tolerate the fact that I was fat, and I couldn't understand why God let me stay that way.

We live on a farm just outside the city. In the summer evenings toward dusk, I'd go down by the pond where it was peaceful and quiet. I could hear the leaves rustle in the wind and the raspy croaks of the frogs all around. I would sit there with my Bible open and pray that God would change me so people would notice me.

But no one did. Every Friday night as I sat at home, I pictured Laura out having a good time at a game or on a date. I began seeing her as the most selfish and snobbish person I'd ever known. I wanted her to pay attention to me, but she wouldn't. So, I began hating her.

During a holiday vacation from school, I went to a Campus Life convention, sponsored by Youth for Christ. There I attended a seminar called "I Am a Worm." I didn't know what it was about, but the seminar was on self-acceptance and I was sick of hearing self-

image pitches. I just doodled and daydreamed until it was over, but the thought came to me that maybe I was afraid to listen because if what they said was right I would have to admit that I really didn't like myself. The thought scared me.

I asked one of the staff leaders for help and he told me an analogy of a painting. He said that I was a picture, and God was the artist who was working on me. He said I could like myself for what I would become as God continued working with me. That comforted me somewhat, but I still had doubts. God wasn't answering my prayers. He didn't appear to be working in me—I still held him responsible for the way I was.

Then one day my aunt told me about Weight Watchers, a club for people who want to lose weight. I was desperate. I had done everything else to lose weight—nothing worked. At her insistence, I decided to give it a try.

The very next meeting I was there along with about 60 others. I waited in a long line of people—some as young as 9 or 10, some as old as 60—all being weighed to see if they had lost or gained any pounds since the last meeting. When I was weighed I was shocked. Right then I resolved to make it work for me, whether God helped or not.

Slowly, very gradually, I lost weight. My parents were very encouraging. They went so far as to eat the same foods I did. And they were pleased with the new disposition I was gaining.

Something else was happening: I was beginning to accept myself. I started feeling more at ease in school. I didn't turn red when I had to get up in front of class to talk. And when I was around others, I found out that people weren't spending their time thinking bad about me. Also, the grudge I held against God dissolved. I saw that he had been waiting all along for me to face my problem and come to him with it. I reached the point of thanking him for making me the way I was and relying on him to continue changing me.

By Christmas my weight goal had been reached! Christmas morning I slipped into a new pair of jeans, sizes smaller than I had ever worn. I can't describe what a terrific feeling that was.

One part of my new life wasn't complete, though. I still had the same old feelings about Laura. I tensed up every time I saw her. She came to Campus Life club meetings occasionally and I felt threatened by that. She had other friends; why did she have to have the attention of my friends, too?

Then came the night of the Campus Life Burger Bash. I didn't want to go because I knew *she* would be there. She was. I didn't have a very good time, and afterward I spent some long hours with the director discussing my problem. Finally, I asked God's forgiveness for hating her.

The next club night I arrived late. The house was quiet as I entered—they were having a time of personal sharing. I took a place in the back of the room, and when it came my turn I just had to volunteer my recent experience of God's forgiveness for the hatred I had felt toward another girl. Laura was there, so I didn't mention her name—I didn't think she'd ever realized my feelings toward her. Later I was approached by one of the staff members who told me that I ought to think about asking the other girl for her forgiveness as well. That scared me a little.

I tried putting it off, but my conscience wouldn't let me, so I prayed for an opportunity to talk to her privately. The next day I watched and waited for an opportunity at school, but I didn't see her. After school I started walking toward the front door and there she was, all by herself, waiting for somebody. I swallowed hard and walked up to her.

"What I have to say is hard . . . I hope you understand. At the meeting Monday night, you were the one I was talking about."

Laura didn't say anything right away. She looked at me evenly and said, "I knew it was me. I just knew it." Then she asked, "Why?"

"Before, I always wanted to be like you and I couldn't understand why it was that I wasn't. I asked the Lord's forgiveness—will you forgive me for having those hate feelings toward you?"

"Oh sure," she said, smiling, and she hugged me then and told me that she loved me. That final barrier was broken. It was the greatest thing in the world. Since then we've become close friends, sharing a common understanding of one another's problems. I know I've become more sensitive to others because I've learned some surprising things about two Lauras. ●

43

by Laura Nash

I was home alone. The house was dark and still—no sounds or voices. A terrible feeling of loneliness came over me—I just had to talk to someone. I picked up the phone and dialed a number; I don't know whose. When a voice came on the other end, I blurted out, "Is—uh—Johnny there?" The voice said, "No, you must have the wrong number," and hung up. I did that a couple of times, but I didn't tell anyone about it.

I suppose I did a lot of things I didn't tell anybody about. I didn't want people to know how messed up and lousy my life really was. I was smoking a little pot and drinking secretly. It was a quiet rebellion.

Then I started getting severe headaches and a nervous stomach. The headaches faded but my stomach problems lingered. I would throw up at odd times, for no reason at all.

The doctor examined me, but couldn't find any real problem. He gave me some pills to take when I started feeling uncomfortable.

When I was alone, I'd feel guilty about what I was doing to myself, and about going against my parents' wishes. They were both Christians and they'd tell me about Christianity. I'd heard it for 17 years. I thought I knew all about it and totally rejected it. I'd scream at them, "I like chocolate cake, but I don't want it crammed down my throat!" My mother would stay up nights praying for me. I didn't think I was that bad.

The school year ended, and all the things I'd looked forward to finally arrived. Summer vacation! Freedom! It was good for a while—parties, drive-in movies, swimming, and sunbathing—but then it got to be a drag. Toward the end of the summer, there wasn't a lot to do. I stayed around home and got into fights with my mother about every little thing: where I was going, the people I was seeing, the kind of bathing suit I wanted to wear.

I got tired of being at home and I heard about the trip to Wyoming that Campus Life was sponsoring. I had been to their meetings and I didn't think much of them, but the mountain climbing, rafting the rapids, and being with other kids sounded fun, so I decided to go.

I had always thought Christian kids were duds—the reason they were Christians was because they didn't have anything else going for them. Christianity, as far as I was concerned, was a long list of dos and don'ts. I was too "neat" for anything like that.

But at that camp in Wyoming, for the first time I took a hard look at my life. I examined the other kids—comparing. I saw they were at peace with themselves and had love for other people. They were open to me and I found I could be open with them. I didn't talk much, but I listened when they shared themselves with me. By the end of the trip, I knew God was where it was at. I wanted to become a Christian then, but I made up my mind to wait until I got home and see if it was real and would stay with me.

Two weeks after I returned home, I called my parents downstairs into the family room in our basement. I turned off the TV and told them I had something to tell them. Not knowing exactly where to begin, I just said, "I want to apologize to both of you for making your lives hell this past year." My mother burst into tears of joy. My father smiled and said, "Laura, we love you. It was worth it to see the way you've changed."

The next week I went to Campus Life club. It was a prayer meeting and a lot of kids were there. I was very self-conscious: there were the people I'd mocked for a year, and I didn't see any reason for them to have anything to do with me. That night I got an uncomfortable feeling as one of the girls—Laura Cheney—told about her struggle with hating another girl. I thought to myself, "That could be me." But I hardly knew her. Why would she hate me?

I didn't think anything else about it until the next day at school. I was sitting on a bench near the entrance to the high school, waiting for some friends, when Laura came up to me. At first I couldn't believe my ears. Was she asking me for forgiveness? I knew she had never really been friendly toward me, but I'd always passed it off—everybody can't be your friend. Then I remembered the feeling of the night before. I told her, "I knew it was me. I just knew it . . . why?" She told me about her problem and asked me to forgive her. I was just a brand-new Christian, and no one had ever trusted me like that before. Immediately I felt love for her. I told her she was forgiven and that I loved her as a friend.

I've thought about it since then: I've never been a person who disliked herself, like Laura. She had those problems to work out. But I had problems too. I had guilt about living like I was and about disappointing my parents. Those were things I faced that she knew nothing about. To her, I was someone who didn't have a care in the world beyond deciding who to go out with, or what I wore to the next party. I was someone who made her life difficult.

But even before I was a Christian, and when Laura was having a hard time, God was working to bring us together! I've grown and so has she. Knowing how God has helped us so much has made us excited about what God can do for anyone. ●

"Your House is Dirty" Anonymous

For a moment, I was stunned, then angry. "That's just fine, Joan," I said, holding my voice even. "If my housekeeping is not good enough for you, please leave."

She looked away. "I was afraid you would take it like that," she said tearfully. "I only wanted to help you."

Help me!

The past few days flashed through my mind. Monday: Joan and her family had arrived, unannounced, finding me harvesting a huge garden. My welcome had been warm and unrestrained. Tuesday: four extra mouths to feed at every meal; extra dishes to wash; extra effort to keep our four toddlers playing happily. And today: with corn and cabbage and cauliflower still to be prepared for the freezer, I had taken off my apron and gone into the study to prepare my Girls' Club Bible study. Joan had gone back to bed for the morning.

Help me!

I had come home from Girls' Club about 9:30 in the evening, glad at having seen conviction and concern on the faces of my high school girls. And I had found the supper dishes still undone.

Help me!

I could think of a dozen better, more constructive ways she could have helped me. I still could hardly believe that I had just heard her say: "I can't stand it any longer, Sharon. Your house is not just untidy. It's dirty!"

She was so right! But surely a surprise visitor takes potluck! Surely she could see the pressure I was under—harvesting not only my own generous garden but also an outsize plot for my holidaying in-laws! Surely she could sense that I was exhausted from my summer's work in camp and vacation Bible school.

I bowed my head to hide the tears that stung my eyelids and

whispered, half-aloud, "O Lord, give me the grace to learn." I didn't know just how much I had asked for in that short prayer, but in the weeks that followed, I was to have the answer—one that came through a long and painful process.

For until the moment that Joan had said, "Your house is dirty!" I had a picture of myself as a successful city girl turned country woman; a happy mother of two toddlers; a contented wife with a Bible-teaching ministry to young people and women and a developing writing ministry. My summer had been filled with effortless entertaining for housefuls of guests. And while I had never majored in housekeeping, I felt that I hit a pretty fair balance between over-scrupulousness and slovenliness. And now this! "Your house is dirty!" It was image shattering.

Suddenly, I found that the strength which had kept me driving was gone. I collapsed. For several days after Joan left I could hardly get out of bed. Physical exhaustion, certainly, was taking its toll. But underlying my physical weakness I felt utterly shaken, unsure of the adequacy of everything I did. Maybe, after all, I was a poor wife and mother. Maybe my priorities had become jumbled. Maybe I was spending too much time in the study and not enough in the kitchen.

Dave's support was the only thing that kept me going at all. While we both admitted that the house had been neglected in the past few weeks, Dave praised me for the hard work I had put into gardening—a strange, new task for me. And he reminded me that I had undertaken camp and vacation school work with his wholehearted endorsement.

"Joan's just envious of your achievements," he rationalized for me. "All she *can* do is keep house—and she can't stand your success in so many other areas." It was a little woolly bit of comfort that I carried around like Linus' blanket in those days.

But then, a week or two after Joan's visit, I asked Dave to help me move some furniture. He put me off, and when I criticized him, his retort was sharp. "When you keep this house well enough that guests don't have to tell you it's dirty, then you can tell me that I'm shirking." The last prop that had been supporting me was kicked out. Dave, too, was taking Joan's club and beating me with it.

I knew I should forgive Joan. And, honestly, I did. And yet still there was no restoration for me. Her little words had shattered my world. I was ill. My eyes were black-ringed with sleeplessness—something which I had never before struggled with. Now I lay awake night after night, aching for rest, but my mind kept going over the past events, trying to rebuild priorities.

Finally, I made an appointment with my doctor. "There's nothing really physically wrong," he told me. "You're just suffering from nervous exhaustion." And when I came home from town, I had a bottle of tranquilizers.

Throughout those weeks there were two things that especially troubled me. First of all, I was unaccustomed to failure of any kind. And now I had failed in doing what I considered a woman's most important job—being a good "keeper at home." And second, I was knowing another, even more bitter kind of failure. I knew each time I took one of those little blue sleeping pills that I simply did not have the strength to get up and face a day. I was failing to deal with this crisis as a victorious Christian.

It was about six weeks after Joan's visit that I finally faced the whole situation without rationalization and self-justification. Certainly, there had been truth in her accusation. And it was that truth which made her words hurt. As I faced myself honestly, I realized I was hurt because I had been made to see inadequacies which I had been pretending did not exist, or else had been dismissing as unimportant. It came to me gradually, and then with shock waves, that I had been fending off a blow, struggling to protect something which God hated in my life. And it was only when I was too tired, too ill, too weary to struggle any more that I finally let the club come down on what it was intended to hit—my pride.

It was when I finally accepted this that Scripture at last came through to me. "My son, despise not the chastening of the Lord, neither be weary of his correction." I had resisted any application of such passages—for I had been refusing to see that behind the attack was not just Joan, but God. I had to see that as a Christian everything allowed into my life was of God's ordaining. And gradually I could feel different about the whole thing.

The tone of my prayers changed. Instead of saying, "Dear Lord, forgive Joan for wounding me so deeply and give me courage to go on," I was finally able to say, "Thank you, Lord, for using Joan to

49

chasten me." And as I studied the passage in Hebrews 12 on God's dealing with us as with sons, I began to feel a new joy. Along with the bruises there was a song: God was dealing with me as with a son.

How good it was to know that he cared, that he was interested enough in me to discipline me for greater development. I was his! However painfully that assurance might have come to me, it brought with it great joy!

I began to be aware in a new way of the message of John 15. "Every branch that beareth fruit, he purgeth it, that it might bring forth more fruit." God's purpose in allowing this attack became clear to me. He had let me be cut—in order that I might bear more fruit. "OK, Lord," I found myself saying, "I see it now. Thank you for the cutting, the trimming, the purging. Now let there be fruit for your glory."

Now, at last, I was able to look clear-eyed and dry-eyed at the things that Joan had itemized and realize that I was, indeed, trying to do too much. Only pride could make me attempt to be a total success in so many areas. In conference with the Lord, I evaluated my activities and reduced them to those which were potentially fruit-producing.

Dave and I decided that we could afford to hire a high school girl to help me once a week so that I would have more time for studying and writing.

The result has been "more fruit." Barbara, the girl who came to work for me, has definitely committed herself to Jesus Christ. Saturdays have been a time of working and fellowshiping together.

Not long after Barbara began to work for me, her mother came to me for counsel, much upset. A neighbor whom she had befriended and helped had called her a "meddling woman." Personal criticism had cut deep. How I thanked the Lord that I had more than theory to share with Mrs. Williams that night. Now, several months later, Mrs. Williams has decided to move her family from the liberal church in our town to the evangelical fellowship of believers. She, too, is "not far from the kingdom."

The Lord has widened my writing ministry beyond all my expectations—and only He knows the results of the weekly Bible teaching column which was published by a local paper, and of the short stories and articles which I have written.

Strange, isn't it. I had heard of the chastening of the Lord. But I had never realized that the rod might be held by a friend. One day soon, I am going to write a letter: "Dear Joan, I want to thank you. . . ." ●

In Life—
Or Death— He
Loves Me by Sharon Fischer

I left the doctor's office in tears and with my head spinning. Only days before, I had begun classes at California State College in San Bernardino, planning toward a master's degree in political science. At 27, I had just completed five years on the staff of Campus Crusade for Christ and was looking forward to my new challenges in graduate school and a possible career in college teaching.

Now, I learned that the unusual pain and swelling in my abdomen was caused by a very large mass, which my doctor said would have to be removed surgically within two weeks. He called a nearby hospital to order tests that afternoon and arranged an appointment for me the next day with a gynecologist.

What would I do about my classes? What about the job I had started just 10 days earlier?

As I drove to the hospital for the tests, I gathered my thoughts. I decided that recuperation from the surgery would take six weeks at the most. I would resume classes in the spring and everything would return to normal. Back in control, I was rather proud of my plans.

But a few days after the operation I was told the news: the "large mass," the size of a football when the surgeons removed it, was a rare type of malignant ovarian tumor. Effective treatment for this particular cancer had been in existence only two years, and research was being conducted at just a few places around the country.

The University of California at Los Angeles was one of those research centers. My doctors told me I needed to go to the UCLA Medical Center the following week to begin chemotherapy treatments in an attempt to halt growth of unseen malignant cells that might be lingering in my body.

In a matter of hours, my life for the next nine months was laid

out: I would return to UCLA every four weeks for four days of chemotherapy; after several months a second exploratory surgery would take place. I was given a 60 percent chance of survival if more growth was found.

Suddenly I realized that my neat little plan for returning to school was not going to materialize. It might be a year before I could resume classes. Or I might not live to resume classes.

Over the next days I grappled with basic questions about my life, my dreams and ambitions, my practical need to earn a living and, most of all, my relationship with God. I knew I had important choices to make about my belief in the goodness of his character, and these choices would influence my response to whatever happened in the coming weeks and months.

In a sense, God had prepared me the preceding year for this situation by helping me gain fresh perspectives on his love. During that time, I was impressed by several people who seemed to enjoy their relationship with him. In essence, each had a real friendship with God, filled with the same relaxation in feeling accepted that the best of human friendship and love offers. Also, the music of B. J. Thomas influenced me to seek fulfillment in a simple, day-to-day relationship with God based on gratitude and acceptance of his love.

So, as I lay in the hospital, even as I wrestled with questions about God's sovereignty—how could he allow this to happen to me?—my thoughts kept returning to what I had been learning of his character: In him resided no evil intent for my life; he was ultimately, sacrificially concerned for my very best; he is a God of pure, unselfish love; and this situation was a real, if mysterious, expression of his love.

I left the San Bernardino hospital for my first treatment at UCLA with this foundational acceptance of God's love. But chemotherapy is not pleasant, nor is living with cancer easy. As the months of treatment have progressed, repeatedly I have been tempted to doubt God's love. In the process, I have learned that to experience God's love I must believe his love. The Apostle John stressed this when he wrote, "And we have come to know and have believed the love which God has for us." Though his love toward us is constant, often it is not experienced because we're too busy doubting it!

My first test in believing God's love was during my first week of

54

chemotherapy, when the continuous nausea so often associated with such treatments hit me. One afternoon I lay in my bed after a particularly difficult bout with nausea, determined to hold on to the truth of God's love for me and not to think ill of him simply because of what I was experiencing. I reflected on all that Christ endured on the cross because of love for me, and, as I realized he had suffered more than I, I truly sensed comfort and understanding from him. Believing his love helped me to experience it at a crucial moment.

How can we make a habit of believing God's love even amid adverse circumstances? One way is to realize that it will be proven in the long run; his loving purposes are not always revealed immediately. For me, trusting God's love has meant commitment to believing it no matter what situation I'm in—sometimes by claiming what the Bible says about it; sometimes by recalling past experience where he has proven his faithfulness.

This commitment was tested when I came face-to-face with financial insecurity, physical discomfort, uncertain future goals, and the emotional upset of packing every fourth week to go to a strange hospital in a huge city. I had a hard time seeing the purpose behind it all.

Thinking through these problems one day, I came across a passage in Psalms that seemed to confirm my need not to give up on God too soon: "Bless our God, O peoples, and sound his praise abroad, who keeps us in life, and does not allow our feet to slip. For thou hast tried us, O God; thou hast refined us as silver is refined. Thou didst bring us into the net; thou didst lay an oppressive burden upon our loins. Thou didst make men ride over our heads; we went through fire and through water; yet *thou didst bring us out into a place of abundance*" (66:8–12).

The promise in the last phrase of the passage helped me realize that I would be the one to lose out if I judged God's love and commitment to me by the apparent limitations of my circumstances—giving up on him before he has the opportunity to reveal his total plan.

Another practical way of believing God's love is to make a daily choice. I learned this lesson about three weeks after my surgery and first chemotherapy treatment, when the hair on my head began to fall out, another side effect of chemotherapy.

On the first day that my hair began to come out in noticeable amounts I realized that my theoretical views of God's love were about to be tested on a very personal level. As I stood in front of my mirror, I burst into tears. Then I put a favorite B. J. Thomas song on the stereo, "Everything always works out for the best/If I have your love, then the world can have the rest."

At that moment, I felt God understood my tears completely, but he was also quietly promising that even this would in some way eventually work out for the best—his and mine. By choosing to believe his love on a daily basis, I experienced special comfort and reassurance.

Finally, the complex issue of physical healing has taught me about believing God's love. I do have the faith to believe that he is able to remove all the cancer from my body and that he is powerful enough to keep it from returning, and I pray for this.

But I have learned that, to believe God's love, I must trust his wisdom, desiring even above healing for him to be glorified through my life, and leaving it up to him to choose how that will best be done.

His glorification may come through miraculous, complete, sudden healing; it may come through the difficulty of continual, drawn-out chemotherapy and more surgery; it may be through taking me home to be with him. As hard as it is to accept some of these options, because I have given him my life, I recognize his prerogative to do with me what he sees best—reassured in the knowledge of his unsurpassed love for me.

As I have applied these principles of believing God's love and have experienced his care in so many ways, I'm reminded of the closing thoughts of Psalm 66: "Come and listen, all you who fear God; let me tell you what he has done for me. . . . Praise be to God, who has not rejected my prayer or withheld His love from me!"

(A few weeks after Sharon wrote this article, exploratory surgery revealed no cancerous growth. Doctors scheduled only two more chemotherapy treatments.—Ed.) ●

When I Wandered from God by L. V. Campbell

I never wanted to wander from God, yet it happened. And it took a horrifying experience to bring me back.

Becoming a Christian had been marvelous and real. I felt joyous, complete, and peaceful. Eager to assume the responsibilities of a Christian, I dived into activity at New Hope Church in Northeast Missouri. Willing to serve, I taught Sunday school, tithed every paycheck, and shared my faith often. I prayed and read my Bible each day. My relationship with God, my church, and my fellow Christians was personal, kindly, and warm. I began to drift from God almost as soon as I moved away from home. How gradually, how unconsciously it happened.

"Are you praying and reading the Bible?" my parents sometimes asked. I didn't tell them. My roommate was not a Christian, so I was not about to kneel and pray as I used to. Instead I lay in bed and prayed. My life was so full and active that usually I fell asleep as soon as a few words whispered through my tired mind. Little by little, I gave up. There were so many exciting things to read that eventually I neglected the familiar Scriptures.

"Are you going to church?" my former minister would ask. I wasn't. Sunday was the greatest day of the week for my new friends and me. Every Sunday morning found us up early for a day of exploring, hiking, driving, swimming. "Well," I told myself, "after all, I can worship God in the world around me." And wasn't Sunday a day of rest? We usually ended the day around a campfire. Conversation flew, but I never spoke to God. I listened to new and far-out ideas, challenging and engrossing to me.

For weeks and months, I took my relationship to God for granted and thought about him less and less. Then it happened. I was riding in a motorboat on the Lake of the Ozarks one Sunday afternoon in

July 1968. A friend, Nikki, was waterskiing behind. She was very good, swinging wide in a graceful arc, performing beautifully, waving and laughing at us in the boat. When we saw the other boat cutting across her path, it was already too late. She screamed and threw her hands protectively over her head. Then she crashed into the boat with a sickening thud.

Instantly we leaped into the water. Nikki wasn't unconscious, but she couldn't help herself. We gently floated her to shore and eased her onto a bed of towels. A boat of white-faced people passed before we reached the beach. They went for an ambulance.

Nikki lay face up, trying to focus her eyes on our worried faces.

"Am I hurt? Am I hurt?" she gasped.

"I think you're all right," someone assured her cautiously.

"There's not a break, not even a cut that I can see," I told her.

"But I feel so funny," she said.

"Where do you hurt?" I asked anxiously.

"I don't hurt. I don't feel anything. But I feel so strange, though. I'm scared. What if I die?"

Her eyes pleaded desperately with us. My friends looked puzzled and embarrassed. Then I noticed blood trickling under her wet hair. Lightly I touched her head. It moved in my hand. It was no longer firm. Her skull had been crushed.

"*Someone* should be able to help me. What if I die?" she repeated faintly.

"Nikki, are you a Christian?" I asked awkwardly.

"No, I guess not."

"Do you want to be? Do you want to belong to God?"

"Why, sure, I guess I do."

"You know that God says you are a sinner," I began.

"Oh, cut it out, clown! Be serious. You sure can't help me." She grinned feebly.

Men with a stretcher came racing up. We hurried to our car and followed the ambulance to the nearest hospital. We rushed into the emergency room to ask about Nikki.

"I'm sorry," the nurse said. "The young lady was dead on arrival."

I was numb. I hardly remember the drive to my place. Once there I fell on my knees and tried to pray. I couldn't. It had been so long. A few stereotyped phrases came, but they meant nothing. The sense

59

of God was no longer with me. An awful feeling of being cast out struck me. Had I been the person I should have been, I could have told Nikki of Christ. Because of the careless way I'd lived, she could not take me seriously. I'd failed God. I'd failed Nikki.

"Please, dear God, help me!" I prayed over and over. And I knew that he would. He had promised. I prayed on and on. As Job, I asked for help; as David, I begged for forgiveness. I was the prodigal son, pleading to come home. And God answered my prayer. His immeasurable love flooded over me. I knew Christ had touched me, for the panic and futility in me changed to hope and peace. When I finally rose from my knees, I knew God was living in me. I had traveled the long way back.

I wish I could say that all has been bright since that night. I can't. We reap what we sow. My careless habits, forged over months, have been hard to break. It has been difficult to pray, to attend church, to study the Bible. My new way of life has clashed with activities of my old friends. Some of them have laughed and ridiculed me. Some have been angry. I have been hurt. My witness for Christ is of little value to them.

I will never again forget Christ's parable of the sprouted seed which died from lack of nourishment. I nourish my spiritual self with prayer, work, study. I share my faith when I can, being ready to witness of Jesus when I sense a spark of interest. I try to make my life an example of the purity and vitality of Christian faith. I don't want ever again to wander from God. ●

Left Behind, But Not Alone by Marie Little

In July, 1975, my world collapsed when my husband Paul was killed in a car collision. Then a truth I had understood only vaguely leaped to life: Christians are not exempt from struggle and pain. There isn't a higher plane "good" Christians reach, surrounded by some plastic bubble free from all difficulties.

I also made another discovery: God had graciously prepared me for the difficult days ahead. A year or more before the accident we had been working and living in Switzerland. Paul had more demands on his time than he could fill. Where did God want him? Which of five or six paths should he take? Both of us and our two teenagers needed to know God's will.

To find guidance, we began reading the book Jeremiah each morning. Jeremiah had a lot of wisdom for us. To our open hearts, God brought a myriad of promises.

Three lessons especially became my foundation stones: God is listening; God has plans for good; God is answering. All came from Jeremiah 29:10–12.

God says, "When you pray, I will listen" (29:12, TLB). Have you ever answered the phone and there was no one at the other end? Or have you ever spoken to your husband and from his "Uh-huh, uh-huh" you knew he wasn't listening? God is not an overworked, preoccupied Father. He concentrates on every word.

"In those days, when you pray I will listen. You will find me when you seek me, if you look for me in earnest. Yes, says the Lord, I will be found of you" (29:12, 13). Seeking the Lord is not merely a quickie, "God bless Mother, Father, Sister, Brother, Amen." It takes earnestness and quietness of heart.

Nor is seeking the Lord chanting a mystical mantra. God is a person, not a force. He thinks, cares, loves, acts. We can commune with him because we are made in his likeness and image.

From Jeremiah 29:11 we learned a second lesson. "I know the plans I have for you, says the Lord. They are plans for good and not for evil to give you a future and a hope." The weight of this hit us squarely. He had a place for us?

We may secretly ask, "Does God really know best?" A young girl thinks he can't possibly choose her mate. A mother schemes to railroad God into her child's life. Each is saying in effect, "You are not totally adequate, Lord."

Jeremiah 10:23 penetrates to the root: "It is not within the power of man to map his life. . . . Correct me, Lord; but please be gentle." There is no circumstance where God has lost control. When the Lord Jesus went to the garden, he prayed that he be delivered from the cross, yet that cross made him the Redeemer of the world.

A special gift to me was the publication of my husband's article, "The God Who Never Lets Things Just Happen," one month before he went to heaven. He explained how the Apostle Paul, in prison for two years on a false charge, says it is for his good and the furtherance of the gospel. It was as if my husband were saying to me that this was the way I should look at each circumstance. "Nothing happens by accident," he concluded his article. "And we can rest with confidence in that."

I could never imagine the Lord of all the earth saying my husband's mansion was not ready because he came unexpectedly. The gates were certainly swung wide open at God's appointed time.

The third lesson we found was in Jeremiah 29:10. "I will come to you and do for you all the good things I have promised." God is answering. This promise gives us faith. In his last few weeks my husband echoed and re-echoed the phrase, "Remember God is working."

"God is answering" means I can have faith even while waiting. The answer may be in process, waiting for changes to be made in me or in another person. He will help me to hold onto him in faith.

"God is answering" means I can have faith that he will direct my praying.

"God is answering" means I can have faith in him to give me wisdom. The Holy Spirit will direct me to the Scriptures for the answer.

As the summer drew near, we planned a vacation to Canada, yet we felt some uncertainty. For three days my husband spent most of his spare time asking the Lord for direction. Then he came into the kitchen and told me to read Ezekiel 12:3. I was stunned as I read, "Pack your bags and go!" Confident of God's direction, we started toward Canada. Five days later Paul graduated into heaven.

When the news came, I sat on the sofa with friends from next door and started to pray. Spontaneously I gave thanks to the Lord for all the love and blessings we had known in the past. It had become such a pattern to expect good from him that it was the most natural thing for me to do in this extremity.

Later the flood of grief swept over me. God gave three more stones to rest on.

The first came in the early morning the day after the accident. "He guards all that is mine" (Ps. 16:5, TLB). My family, my future, my occupation, my finances, and all of the unanticipated events ahead were under his protection. I could relax in his care.

Of course, I immediately asked why I hadn't gone with him, why the other lane of traffic hadn't been empty, why it had to be such a large Ford LTD that hit our Volkswagen. He assured me: "I could have done any of these things. It was not my will." That was enough. I knew I couldn't ask that question again. I could pour out my hurt and pain and sorrow, but I could never question his wisdom.

The second promise was, "Thou wilt shew me the path of life: in thy presence is fulness of joy" (Ps. 16:11). I saw that at this stage in my life, as always, he wanted me to overcome and be a whole, restored person. A grieving person needs to cry, but then she needs help to stop crying. Grief and sorrow bring darkness and paralysis. Lying on my bed the day of the funeral, I opened to Jeremiah to remind myself of God's word to us. My mind wondrously cleared. I felt lightened. His word brought light. The path of life was upward, not toward collapse.

At a conference with the Billy Graham team, I met a godly gentleman who had prayed for us for many years. His only word to me was, "Are you Marie Little? I have a verse for you." He simply quoted, "Now may the God of hope fill you with all joy and peace in believing, that you may abound in hope, through the power of the Holy Spirit" (Rom. 13:15, NASB).

I listed the attributes he wanted for me. Joy. Peace. Hope. Fullness of joy. I knew this was his direction for me. If I went any other way, I was not in the path he had planned. This knowledge kept me from giving in on many occasions.

The third promise came from Ps. 104:34: "My meditation of him shall be sweet: I will be glad in the Lord." A new knowledge of the sweetness of his presence had overwhelmed Paul and me in the early morning vigils with the Lord through the book of Jeremiah. Now I came to him, urgently needing that sweetness.

Remarkably, this was repeatedly confirmed to me in new promises. "Day by day the Lord also pours out his steadfast love upon me, and through the night I sing his songs and pray to the God who gives me life" (Ps. 42:8, TLB). He knew how hard the evenings and nighttimes would be. Loved poured out on me? A song in the night? A sheer miracle, indeed.

As time went on, this sweetness and love and joy became the only source of deliverance from the half-physical, half-emotional pain deep within and beyond any human touch. I knew what it was like to eat a very bitter or peppery food. Quickly I would have to find a sweet to counteract the burning. While meditating on him I could become truly and genuinely glad. The only cure for sorrow is the sweetness of the presence of the Lord. That sweetness counteracts all hurt.

Finally, in hours of deepest loneliness and struggle I can offer these trials to him as a sacrifice. What does he do with them? As he promises in Isaiah 61:3, he gives beauty for ashes, the oil of joy for mourning, and the garment of praise for the spirit of heaviness. Beauty, joy, praise—he is the companion of the bereaved. ●

Dilemmas in a Factory by Clarence Trowbridge

Like millions of Americans, I work in a factory. I share certain problems with other workers, but I have other problems that arise because I am a born-again Christian. You might better understand what these problems are if I told you about some friends of mine. Let's call them Christians A., B., C., and D.

When Christian A. was first assigned to the milling department in a certain factory, he was put to work with another man on the same machine. Theoretically the machine required two operators, but only theoretically. The fact was it scarcely required one.

After the instruction period the co-worker notified Christian A.: "I'm going to take a nap back of the machine. If the foreman asks where I am, tell him I went to the washroom or something, then come back and wake me up."

The co-worker took his nap, and sure enough the foreman did come around and asked where he was.

Christian A. felt a little sick. What should he do? The name of Christ might be cursed if the co-worker lost his job because of telling the truth, yet neither was it right to lie. Trapped, he chose to do what most Christians would have done in similar circumstances. He lied.

Down deep inside, Christian A. based his decision on two known facts: God forgives; man does not. These facts prompted his decision though he may never have fully realized it.

If you think this example is farfetched, the chances are that you do not work in a factory.

Take another illustration, that of Christian B., who works in a chemical factory. When he was hired he determined to do his very best on the job. But after work on his third day he was met by a sour-looking delegation of men who told very plainly the way they felt about it.

"What do you think you're doin', wise guy?" "You tryin' to ruin things for everybody?" "Look, from now on you better get real slow!" "We don't like guys like you around here." And so on.

They left him with this problem. Should he buck these men or lay down on the job?

Or take Christian C. He has been working at the same dairy for a number of years. He is very well liked, and has always tried hard to be an "all-right guy." His trouble was that he succeeded too well. One day a friend and fellow worker came to him with a casual request:

"Say, old pal, I have to leave early tonight, so I stuck my card behind yours. Punch me out as you leave, will you?" And he turned on his heel and was gone.

Christian C. was on the horns of a dilemma. Should he punch the man's time card in violation of company rules, or refuse and stand to lose the man's friendship?

The one complicating factor in these three situations is this: these Christian men wanted to remain on good terms with their fellow workers in order to reach them with the gospel. This desire is the underlying idea of 1 Corinthians 9:22: "I am made all things to all men, that by all means I might save some."

The difficulty arises in distinguishing right from wrong while remaining friends with the unsaved.

Some say that you should ask yourself the question, "What would Jesus do?" then do it.

Let us examine the case of Christian D., who began to witness to a fellow employee on their ten-minute coffee break. So interested did the man become in what he had to say that Christian D. found himself still witnessing some ten minutes after the coffee break was over. The man was obviously under deep conviction, and Christian D. was faced with a real decision. Should he continue to witness, hoping for a decision, on time they both owed to the company? Or should he return to work immediately, thereby losing an excellent opportunity that might never come again?

"What would Jesus do?" Frankly, Christian D. didn't know. And the chances are, many another Christian wouldn't know either.

To complicate things further, the Christian in the factory must make all his decisions in an atmosphere that is hardly conducive to godliness or right-mindedness. The air is often blue with language indescribably foul. And I know I am not the only Christian who has had to work in a room papered with pictures of nudes.

The union may also complicate the Christian's problems. In theory, as a democratic organization it is good for the union to have the Christian help mold its policy. But in some cases he may find that the union upholds inefficiency, deceit, and even disobedience of certain company rules.

The union may also insist on low work output in order to protect certain unionists who do not wish to work any harder. The idea that worker efficiency and higher pay scales might go hand in hand is often regarded as "bunk."

In companies that have a paid sick leave clause it is common for most of the men to "get sick for a week." When the company eventually seeks release from such a provision the blame is likely to fall on the honest minority who did not draw sick leave. Ridiculous, you say? It happened to me.

These are real problems, just a few out of many. And no one could pretend to have solved all the unique problems that arise from factory employment. I think, however, that I have found a workable formula which may be of value to some Christian who is meeting these situations constantly and wondering if there are principles to guide him. It's a formula found in 1 Corinthians 16:13, 14:

"Be always on your guard; stand firm in your faith; keep on acting like men; continue to grow in strength; let everything be done in love." (Williams trans.)

For convenience I have reworded this formula into three rules:
1. Make an open stand for Christ.
2. Adopt an uncompromising attitude.
3. Temper all your actions with love.

These rules are completely interdependent; you must abide by all three or none at all.

By making a stand for Christ I mean letting your fellow employees know openly that you are a Christian. The reason for this is that many of the problems such as we have been discussing result from a Christian trying to live on a high moral plane without first letting his fellow workers know the reason why.

Your fellow employees must understand that you *are* a Christian before you try to live like a Christian. If you fail to do this your good behavior will be put down either as spitefulness or just plain orneriness by the other workers.

I am not saying that a man cannot be a Christian without making an open issue of it. Indeed, I think that the majority of Christians are trying to do just exactly that. I have seen many of these "secret" Christians.

I will say that any attempt to live the Christian life in a crowded factory will end in defeat and heartache if the Christian will not take a stand for Christ. The temptations will come at the secret Christian so thick and fast that his head will fairly spin.

By making a stand and sticking to it, the Christian automatically short-circuits many temptations. Once the unsaved men understand your position they will often decide for themselves that a thing is wrong for you and never even present it to you for a decision. For example, a man who had considered asking you to help him steal something from the plant (a time-honored custom in many places) may decide beforehand that you wouldn't do it, and not bother asking.

If he has the gall to ask you anyway, it will be easier for you to say no because he will know that you are refusing on purely moral grounds and not because you have anything against him personally.

Again, if you leave the room when the language becomes too sickening they will look at one another and nod—but they'll understand.

When you bow your head over your lunch bucket the men will know what you are doing, and only the meanest will try to bother you. In fact, if some crass individual does decide to have some fun at your expense while you are praying he may find to his astonishment that he himself has incurred the disapproval of the men. For even the most black-hearted sense that there is something wrong in disturbing a man who is talking to God.

If your stand is open enough you may find that it becomes almost unnecessary to "preach the gospel." You will become an "epistle, known and read of all men."

Moreover, you will find the unsaved coming to you. They will often seek you out whenever they think they can have a word with you in private. At first their questions may concern factual things

69

like ethics and Bible truths. It is their way of finding out whether or not you will be able to answer their questions.

Later, when their confidence in you has increased, they will come out with the real question that has been troubling them. If ever a Christian has a God-given chance to testify for Christ, it is at that time.

Moreover, a Christian must adopt a firm, uncompromising attitude. This at times may tax all the determination and courage a man has. Once having made a decision based on the Bible or on what he knows to be right, the Christian must never go back on it or change it to meet changing circumstances. Painful and hard as this may be, it will spare him even greater pain in the future.

For one thing, make it a habit to always tell the truth. Lies are no longer considered sins when told within the confines of a factory. The problem of Christian A. was of this type. Yet the problem should never have been allowed to rear its ugly head. At the other man's first suggestion of a nap the Christian should have taken a firm stand and made it clear that he *could not* lie for him.

This might have angered the man a little, but not half as much as if Christian A. sent the foreman back to wake him up—which was really the proper thing to do, as the situation developed.

Christian B. already had this attitude, and he continued to put out a day's work for a day's pay in spite of the warning. He was also careful to avoid an "I'll show them" attitude. Now—less than a year later—most of the resentment has died down and Christian B. enjoys an envied reputation as a hard worker. When a man needs a work partner he is apt to choose Christian B., because he knows that Christian B. will make his own job easier.

In this latter case it eventually became clear that the resentment did not arise from the majority of the men but from a comparatively small group of "leeches." These men are vocal and usually pose as ardent unionists, simply because their kind needs the strongest possible union to keep the lot of them from getting fired for laziness.

Christian C. should have nipped his problem in the bud by stopping his friend and politely refusing to punch his card. If necessary he should even have run after him. This would have been awkward, but not nearly as awkward as the situation in which he allowed himself to become involved.

The problem of Christian D. is not so easy to answer, and I approach it cautiously. Certainly there are times when a man must take his orders from the Holy Spirit, and follow them unmindful of the consequences. At times every Christian must say as Paul said, "Necessity is laid upon me; yea, woe is me, if I preach not the gospel!" (1 Cor. 9:16)

Nevertheless, in my judgment, in the absence of a Spirit directive to the contrary it is better to gently leave off witnessing and return to work. We can be sure that the Holy Spirit will not leave off his work but rather will continue to work in the man's heart until there is a better opportunity to speak with him.

But it is the spirit of love that makes much of this possible. The firm, unyielding stand of the separated Christian seems very harsh at times. Only the *loving nature* of the born-again Christian can soften that harshness and reveal to the world that we are friendly and kind and sympathetic to their problems.

These three rules taken from Paul's first letter to the Corinthians will enable the Christian to live a life consistent with the faith he professes.

It must be admitted that they will have little effect on the obscene pictures on the wall or the vile language that beats upon his ears. Since there may be no escape from these things physically, it is necessary to develop an inner protection against them.

If your work is largely mental you can preoccupy your mind with it. However, if your work is largely manual it would be well to cultivate a sort of mental preoccupation with the things of Christ. Since my own job is manual labor I can suggest a few devices that will help.

A favorite hymn or gospel song hummed over and over will tend to hang on all day with its message of hope or praise. Or you might memorize a verse of Scripture on the way to work, and all day long try to plumb its depths of meaning. Attack it from all angles and try to exhaust all the truth in it. But this third device I like best of all: take the offensive and tell the man next to you just what Jesus means to you! ●

Those Deep Down Illnesses by Bernard Ramm

"**I**f a person is a new creation in Christ, doesn't that cure all his emotional problems?"

"Don't Christians have nervous breakdowns because Satan is trying to ruin their ministry?"

These are typical remarks of Christians concerning faith and psychotherapy. Do they constitute real insight or are they built upon misconceptions?

Let us begin with an observation in two parts:

1. Many people who are confirmed atheists are well-adjusted, happy, and contented, psychologically speaking. If lack of a wholesome religious experience were at the root of neurosis, then all atheists should be neurotic, but they obviously are not.

2. Many Christians with a vital experience of Christ and a persistent devotional life with daily confession of sin have deep-seated emotional problems and may be found in mental hospitals. If Christianity were the emotional cure-all some Christians represent it to be, then any emotionally disturbed Christian is a hopeless backslider or a wicked sinner. However, anyone who has had any experience with emotionally disturbed Christians knows that this is not necessarily true.

If atheism does not always produce neurosis or serious mental illness, and if religion does not necessarily cure it, then we must look elsewhere for the relationship of emotional disturbance and Christian experience.

Regeneration and emotional integration operate on two different levels; therefore, they may or may not influence each other. This explains why an atheist can have emotional integration of the healthy sort but no regeneration. His lack of faith does not make him emotionally sick. The Christian has spiritual regeneration and therefore wholeness.

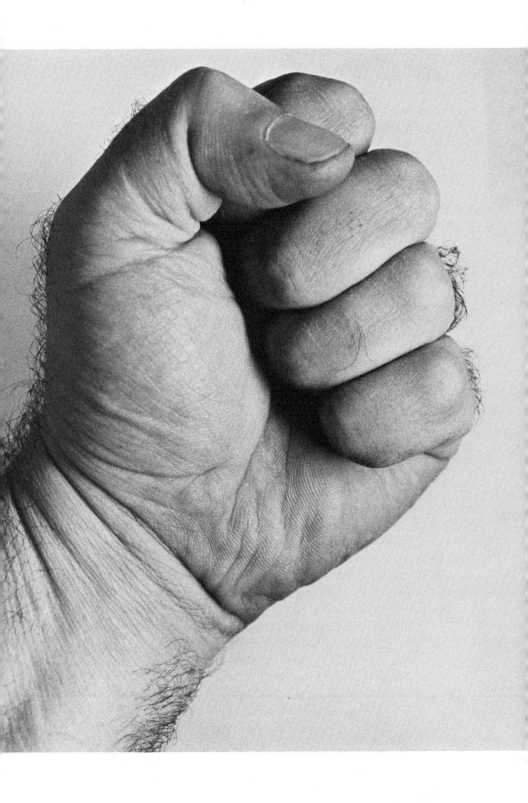

It is confusing to Christians when the same self that believes has emotional problems; therefore good Christians sometimes imply that if an emotionally sick person had enough spirituality he would be cured of his neurosis.

I am not saying that our emotions and our faith are in watertight compartments. An atheist in depression might go into deeper depression because he is an atheist, whereas a Christian with a poor self-image may find help in Christian faith. But, generally speaking, emotional integration and regeneration operate at relatively different parts of the self and this we need to explore.

Emotional integration concerns the way we handle the problem of existence—stress, self-image, self-identification, interpersonal relationships, bodily needs, self-needs, and sexuality. These problems begin the day we are born. As the child is faced with problems ranging from the need for food to the need for parental love, he develops mechanisms (I use this term broadly for all sorts of methods the self develops, intellectually or bodily, to satisfy its complex needs) for problem solving. By the time he is a teenager his basic mechanisms for handling the stress of life have been quite concretely set.

Spiritual conversion is an act of faith or repentance, through conviction of gospel truth by the Holy Spirit. By the time conversion occurs, a person has been developing patterns of handling life's emotional problems for a number of years.

Two things are apparent at this point:

1. The act of faith and conversion comes at a higher, more profound level than emotional integration.

2. By the time a person can make an intelligent act of faith he has already had many years of developing and learning mechanisms to handle his everyday problems.

Psychologists offer various explanations for man's emotional problems, but one explanation that makes sense to me is based on mechanisms and attitudes.

Let us call all the means and methods, healthy or unhealthy, for solving life's problems "mechanisms." And let us call the rich complex of faith, conviction, repentance, and new life in Christ an "attitude"—the Christian position toward life.

With this distinction in mind, it can be seen how mechanisms and attitudes may function at different levels. In some dramatic conversions a change in attitude has had a profound change in mechanism, as seen in the case of some alcoholics. But it does not necessarily follow.

A person with healthy mechanisms may get along well with people but ignore God. A Christian with healthy attitudes may not have overcome warped mechanisms.

I am not denying that for the new creation in Christ "all things are become new." I am not denying the power of the indwelling Holy Spirit of Romans 8, transforming man's moral nature. But what I am saying is that just as a new convert with a partially paralyzed or withered hand may need continued physical therapy, so a new convert with a withered emotional reaction toward life may need psychological therapy.

How do you react to an invitation to an unusual social occasion? How do you react to a supposed "cold shoulder" given you at church? How do you react to frustration, defeat, or criticism?

Whether you withdraw or meet the challenge head-on, whether you repress your emotions or depreciate yourself, whether you rationalize or tend to make mountains out of molehills is determined initially by your established mechanisms. If any of these reactions get out of hand, you're in trouble emotionally.

Is there no correlation of mechanism and attitude? Yes, there is, as long as the ego-mechanisms are open to the spirit-attitudes. To the extent to which this contact exists, the Christian has resources which help reform his unhealthy mechanisms.

For example, people with emotional ills almost always depreciate themselves. The counselor or psychiatrist does his best to rebuild the person and to eliminate his perpetual self-depreciation. A Christian who can develop strong attitudes about himself through prayer, study of Scripture, and other devotional activities may accomplish some of this by himself.

Or depression may exhibit itself as a lack of purpose and meaning in life. If a Christian gets a new purpose in life through Christ and establishes new appreciations of what life is all about in such concepts as "For me to live is Christ," he may correct his faulty mechanisms.

Where do these unhealthy mechanisms come from? Society is

sinful in many respects; even Christian parents are sinners. Those who surround the young infant and child may be devout Christians and have the best intentions in the world. But they may not give their children the best methods of coping with the problems of life. Instead, they may unwittingly and unconsciously build weak mechanisms into the child.

A healthy faith and the fellowship of a loving church can strengthen one emotionally and build sound methods of handling the stresses of life. In his private devotions, in the reassurances of his faith, and in community of the church, the Christian can find resources for emotional healing that are not open to the nonbeliever. But it is not automatic. ●

My God Is Greater Than Watergate by Charles W. Colson

I grew up in a middle-class town outside of Boston. My humble parents worked hard and my dad went to night school. Whenever he had a little time for me on Sunday afternoons, he would always tell me the same lesson. He'd say, "Chuck, just work hard, work hard. Anything you work at, you can do it."

Well, I burned up the first 40 years of my life trying to prove my dad was right. I had a full scholarship to college; I was the youngest company commander in the Marine Corps; I went on to be the youngest administrative assistant in the United States Senate; I built a law firm from two men to 30 in a short period of time; and then in 1969 President Nixon asked me to come to the White House to be his special counsel. Within the first year I became one of the three or four men who could walk in and out of the Oval Office any day of the week and counsel with the President, the most important man in the world.

The President would call in the middle of the night; I had a phone connected to anywhere in the world; there were limousines and briefing papers and seeing Dr. Kissinger twice a day; and we made decisions that we said would change the course of history for all mankind.

I left the White House after the 1972 election, and I guess I should have been able to look at the 42 years and feel impressed that I had done all those things my dad told me I could do if I really worked.

But I felt a deadness, an emptiness, maybe a depression. The emptiness continued into the spring of 1973 when I went to Boston to be with a man I had known in the 1960's—Tom Phillips. Tom was the president of Raytheon Company, the largest employer in New England. He was a man I could very easily identify with: born of immigrant parents, he worked his way through school at night, became an engineer at Raytheon at 25, a vice president at age 36, and president a couple of years later when the company employed 50,000 people.

I went into his office and found a relaxed Tom Phillips. I had heard from one of his associates that he was involved in religious work and I assumed he was raising money for the church, which is what any president of a large company ought to do for his public image.

So I said, "What's happened, Tom?" Without batting an eye, Tom said, "I've accepted Jesus Christ and committed my life to him."

Well, I could have gone right off that chair. I believed in God. I grew up in a part of the United States which Baptists call the vast Unitarian wasteland of the Northeast, where you heard the Lord's name in church usually only when the janitor tripped over the mop bucket.

I changed the subject in a hurry and soon returned to Washington. That summer was for me a nightmare. In that dark summer, poison flowed through the veins of that city; people couldn't even talk with one another. All those things I'd built into my life that I was so proud of just crumbled around me. All the things Tom Phillips was, Washington wasn't. Every time I talked to him, he had that caring tone in his voice, a genuine concern.

I called Tom and said I'd like to spend some time with him. On a hot summer night on the porch of his suburban Boston home, I said, "Tom, tell me what's happened in your life." Before he said anything, he read to me from a marvelous little paper book titled *Mere Christianity*, by C. S. Lewis. He read from the chapter, "The Great Sin—Pride," about how pride has been the chief cause of human misery from the beginning of time. All the while Tom was reading those eloquent words, parading before my mind's screen were all the scenes out of my life. I felt unclean for the first time in my life, and then Tom told me what had happened to him.

Here was a man who had everything—honorary degrees from colleges he couldn't get into as a kid, six-figure income, stock options, Mercedes in the driveway, big white house in the suburbs, kids in private schools. He had everything but he had nothing enduring.

One night he was in New York and he couldn't get out of the

78

city; his plane was grounded. He wanted something to do, and he went to hear Billy Graham in a crusade meeting. Tom Phillips found that night what he'd been searching for and he walked down the aisle and asked Jesus Christ to come into his life.

He told me this story and I was really moved by it, but I was the big-time Washington lawyer and the Presidential confidant. Tom asked, "Do you want to pray?" Tom prayed, I didn't. I left the house, and when I tried to put the keys into the ignition, I was crying so hard I couldn't start the car. I pulled the car out into the road and sat there alone, asking God with some bumbling prayers to take me. I sat there alone, but maybe really for the first time in my life I was not alone.

My wife Patty and I went off to the Maine coast, and like a good lawyer, I had two columns on my yellow pad: There is a God/There isn't a God; Jesus Christ is God/He isn't God. At the end of four days I had piles of notes, and I made the magnificent discovery that Jesus Christ's claims and promises were true. Words which had sounded so mystical to my ears only weeks before fell so naturally from my lips. I didn't really even tell my wife what had happened.

Well, the press heard about my conversion and it was really uproarious for a while, but all kinds of letters flowed into my office. Part of one read:

"I am a staff sergeant in the United States Air Force. For 19 years I've been trying to find myself. I went to church on several occasions, but the pastors didn't reach me. After reading the article about you, it has helped me more than anything in my entire life. It is Christmas morning. I am usually drunk or trying to get drunk by now, but here I am, watching the children open up their presents, and thinking about going to church somewhere instead of the club or someone's house to get drunk. I didn't even buy any booze this year. It's people like you who confess their past (maybe-not-so-good life—wrongs) or whatever it may be called, sure do help people in a position like me. I truly feel free within my inner self this morning, and I pray that God may help both of us in all of our trying efforts. I am going to try and find that book, *Mere Christianity*, down here and read it myself. God blessing you, S/Sgt. Nathaniel Green."

When I read that letter, I realized it was worth it all. I could look back on the 11 years in some of the highest positions in government service, and in all the executive service, and in all the executive orders and laws I'd tried to write, and not think of one human life I'd changed for the better. And now with my whole life crumbling around me while awaiting imprisonment, I could see a family united, a man freed from 19 years of bondage to whisky.

(In June 1974 Colson was sentenced for one-to-three years in prison for his involvement in the break-in in the office of Daniel Ellsberg's psychiatrist.—Ed.)

It was in prison I found full spiritual freedom. Everything went wrong in my life in January of last year. I didn't believe God had forsaken me, but I also couldn't bring myself, as the Scripture tells us, to praise him for what had happened.

First of all, the other three men who were in prison for Watergate offenses—offenses more serious and with longer sentences than mine—all were released on January 8 last year. On January 8 my wife had to watch on television while the other wives were reunited with their husbands at home. She knew that we still faced maybe two and a half years before we would be back home together. My dad had died while I was in prison, and I couldn't get a furlough because it looked bad to have the publicity, so my mother was alone and ill. I was disbarred from law practice, and I hadn't really expected to be.

And then my lawyer called me and said, "Chuck, are you ready for a tough one? Your son is in jail in South Carolina for narcotics possession." He was my second son, a kid who had never given us a day's trouble, but who had gotten bitter during all the problems of Watergate. I couldn't even ask for a parole to be with him. The worst day of my life was when my son was in jail and I couldn't be with him.

I went back into my little bunk that night and I tried to praise God. I knew I was supposed to and I couldn't do it.

Then I got a telephone call from Congressman Al Quie, my brother in Christ. His voice was kind of hesitant, and he said, "Chuck, I don't quite know how to handle this. I know what you're going through and all your family problems. Chuck, I've found an old statute that says one man can serve another man's sentence, and I'm going down to see my friend the President this afternoon and ask him if I can't come and serve the rest of your sentence."

I put down the phone. There was no talking Al out of that. I went back to my bunk and said, "OK, Lord. You win. If that's what it takes for me to know that I should praise you in all things, if that's what it takes to know your love—one brother for another—well, I praise you. I praise you for my son being in jail."

Two days later the judge who had sentenced me released me from prison on the grounds of what had happened to my son. Since then my son and I have become closer than we ever were before. So I can tell all my brothers and sisters to praise God in all things, because he's got a plan for you. You won't know it at the time, and it may seem pretty tough at the time, but praise him in all things and he will truly set you free.

How does the good news and the love of Jesus Christ spread? One man to one man. We look at the last page of the Bible and we know that the Lord Jesus Christ is with us, that God does have a plan for the nations. So instead of wringing our hands and turning away in despair, let's ask ourselves, "Lord Jesus, am I this day living for you? Are you in control of my life? I want you to be."

And once you have settled that question, then turn to a neighbor and tell him you love him because Jesus loves him. Reach out and touch someone else in love. Watch what can happen when the heart of one man is renewed, and one man touches one man, and a whole nation can feel its spirit lifted.

Then when you go to bed at night, pray that when they write about this era they won't have to say that God's men and women dared not to stand up and be judged and to love one another and to spread the good news of Jesus Christ. ●

God's Other Answer by Malcolm Nygren

There isn't any God. Or if there is, he hates me—and I hate him!"

What brought Louise to this tight-lipped despair? Most of her life had been all that she could want. Reared in a Christian home, she had loving parents who taught her to trust God and have confidence in herself. Later she met the one man in all the world. Art was a kind and thoughtful husband and a loving father. There were three children in a home with affection, and a fourth soon to be born.

Then Art was seriously injured in an accident in the mill where he worked. A phone call brought Louise to the hospital. Art lay in the hissing tubes and machines of the intensive care ward, neither alive nor quite dead. The days dragged on with little change. Louise prayed in the hospital chapel while she waited for her 10 minutes with him every two hours. In the evening she stopped at the church on her way home. Alone in the silent nave, she pressed her forehead against the pew in front of her and prayed, "God, don't take him away from me."

And Art died.

He died, and Louise was left with four children and a mortgaged house and no idea of what to do.

"I prayed and God did nothing," she cried. "What kind of God would do that?"

Most of us have prayed without avail, or at least without the kind of help we desperately wanted. The Apostle Paul did. He prayed to be freed from some nameless physical agony. Three times he prayed, not in his ordinary way, but in petitions so fervent that he numbered and remembered them. Yet he carried this stake impaling his flesh to his grave.

Even the least religious among us pray when we are in trouble. The hospitals hum with prayer. Yet last breaths are still drawn, pulses stop, and the beloved walk away sorrowing, looking back to see if someone is running to tell them it isn't so. We must somehow relate these disappointments to God. For the Christian the question can be faith-shattering: Why does God answer some prayers in the way that they are asked—and not others?

There would be no problem if all prayers were answered or if none of them were. If no prayers were answered, we would only have to accept the fact that life is a machine, processing us through, grinding us out. But the Christian faith denies that unfeeling universe. There are too many witnesses to answered prayer, and each witness raises the question again.

Martin Luther wrote, "Prayer . . . has raised up in our time three persons who lay in danger of death: myself, my wife, and Philip Melancthon in 1540 at Weimar."

Arctic missionary Wilfred Grenfell told how the ice on which he was traveling broke loose from the shore and drifted out to sea. With death before him, Grenfell prayed. Miraculously the wind changed and drove him back to land and to his mission—which eventually peopled the northern wastes with Christians.

Most Christians have personal memories of being rescued in response to prayer. What the unbeliever might dismiss as mere good fortune, the Christian recognizes as the act of a loving God. The power that created and governs the world is not unfeeling, deaf to the entreaties of those who suffer. God hears and cares, and often acts in just the way we hope.

But not always. Luther and his wife and Melancthon are all dead now. Did no one pray when they died? Grenfell died, and there were tears in huts and shelters all across the Arctic. No matter what our own experience in the past, none of us can predict that our next heartfelt prayer will bring just the response that we want. It may. But also, it may not.

What do we do when our dreams are crashing and God doesn't answer our plea that he put them back together again? What can keep our faith from being swept away in the flood of our sorrows? How can we answer the questions that press in on us, questions about God, questions about prayer, questions about what we can dare to hope?

It may be, we think, that we have not prayed in the right way.

Perhaps the prayer must be said by someone with a special gift that we lack. Or maybe we lack the faith to make our prayers work right. We're told that if we only believe that God will answer our prayers, believe without a shadow of doubt, then we will have what we want. But we see the shadows of doubt in the corners of our prayers, and we despair of ever earning his help.

The trouble with that explanation of unfulfilled prayers is that it runs counter both to our experience and to the Bible. Our experience is that our answered prayers have nothing to do with our skill in praying. God has often answered our clumsy prayers, mumbled in hospital corridors in all the wrong words, tumbling out of a heart sick with fear and doubt. A god who demands a magic prayer-formula from us doesn't resemble the One we met in the Bible. Such a god reminds us of those surly trolls of nursery tales, who can be forced to yield our wishes when we say the proper word. This Rumpelstiltskin god is not the God of Abraham, Isaac, and Jacob, the God we know in Jesus Christ. There is no secret trick to prayer, on our side or on God's.

But what kind of God is he then? Who is it that will not always move at our plea to save the happiness of a family, the health of a child, the hopes of the young?

We should ask a different question. In what kind of a world would God move at each of our prayers, healing and helping whenever we asked? It would be a world without tears. There would be no conflict or dying or burden of disappointed hopes. It would be a world far grander and more sublime than the one we know.

The Bible does describe a world like that, where there shall be an end to death, and to mourning and crying and pain. But it is not this world. It is a world with a condition so remarkable that we can barely imagine it: everyone there wills what God wills.

It can't be any other way: a God who filled the prayer-orders of people whose wills were not his own would be no God at all—he would be a heavenly vending machine.

But what is God's will?

The God we meet in Jesus Christ has purposes we can only dimly make out; he is not like anyone we have ever known. "My ways are not your ways," he says (Isa. 55:8, 9), and we weep because we can't understand what his ways are. The distance between God and

84

me is infinitely greater than that between my dog and me. There will always be a large, unexplained remainder in our understanding of what God does.

The answers to prayers that we understand are those that are earthbound, as plain to our understanding as the food bowl is to my dog. We can see and applaud those answers to our prayers that are anchored in this world, their dimensions limited to today and not forever. But God is not limited that way. His most profound responses to us come from eternity. He is the God of living, loving mystery.

Whatever it was that Paul called a thorn in his flesh, he was so harassed by it that he prayed repeatedly for relief. Yet he heard God saying to him, "My grace is sufficient for you, for my power is made perfect in weakness" (2 Cor. 12:9).

God sometimes says: "I will help you bear it." "There is something good for you yet." "I will not leave you," and much more. The answer, "I am enough," is one that comes from eternity and not from next door. We pray from today; God answers us from eternity. He knows that in his time all the sick will be healed, all the lonely will be together again, and all the hurts will stop hurting. He knows that his plans arch out of this world into eternity, and that we can see only this earthly end of the arch. And so God promises to be with us with power to uphold our fainting spirits. Some prayers are answered with action, but all of them are answered with love.

That is enormously important because so often our prayers are about soul-wrenching things. Jesus cried out to be spared the cross, and our own petitions come often out of agony. It is just when suffering must be borne that we most need the companionship of God. When the bereavement must be faced, the pain endured, the unwanted sacrifice made—these are the times when we must not be alone. We are not alone. In those terrible moments, God's grace is enough to bring us through. That is God's other reply to our petitions. It is a promise: that though we suffer we shall not be broken, that he will never forsake us, and because he will not, we shall endure. ●

Confession of a Sinking Preacher by Alan Redpath

I find that Christians of every age group today are involved in a rat race. They're on a conveyor belt from dawn until night seven days a week—too tired to pray, too weary to read the Bible. Studies, business, the family, social life—all these responsibilities produce a feeling that one is beginning to sink.

Beginning to sink . . . what did Peter do in the same circumstances? He cried out, "Lord, save me!" (Matt. 14:30).

That's a very short prayer, but under the circumstances I don't think it could have been much longer. The water was probably up to his chin. He was desperate. "Lord, save me!" It is a confession of need. Faith works most convincingly when there is no other way out!

Afterward Jesus exposed the cause of his sinking—a breakdown in Peter's basic relationship with God. "Wherefore didst thou doubt?" In other words, why has your confidence in God ceased?

When Peter first left the ship to come to Christ, he had no problem with the winds and waves. But when he began concentrating on them, he began to sink. This isn't only Peter's trouble; it's yours and mine. We can give our time and our concentration to battling with life's problems until our spiritual horizons grow dim. We can lose the sense of the presence of the One who has power to control the storm. Then we begin to sink.

But Jesus reversed the defeat when Peter called. Immediately Jesus takes him by the hand and lifts him up. A new power takes over. That's exactly what you need when you're sinking—a Master who can take hold and lift you above the storm and enable you to triumph. Jesus Christ must be Lord. He must take control.

One winter evening a few years ago I was aboard a plane at New York's Kennedy airport, waiting on the runway for the take-off to

Chicago. It was a very foggy night and the snow was falling. I looked out the window and saw four men with their ladders on the wings sweeping away the snow. The whole situation was most uncomfortable. But shortly there was a tremendous roar and that plane gradually took speed. In a flurry of snow it sped along that runway and at the speed of about 150 knots the nose went up in the air and the plane began to soar—eventually to reach 35,000 feet, in a clear, brilliant moonlit night. In less than two hours I was at Chicago's O'Hare Field. What lifted us off the ground and eventually above the very storm itself? At a speed of 150 knots another law came into operation. Until that moment the law of gravity had held that plane on the runway, but the law of aerodynamics began to take over and the thrust of four jet engines overcame the law of gravity and kept it in subjection. The plane soared through the storm.

So it is in the Christian life. "The law of the Spirit of life in Christ Jesus has set me free from the law of sin and death" (Romans 8:2). Hallelujah! When I say, "Lord, save me!" at that very moment he stretches out his hand and lifts me up, and I experience the upward pull of a living Christ.

In 1964 I was preparing my message for a Sunday—it was Saturday afternoon—in my study in Edinburgh. As I was writing it out, I suddenly lost control of my hand and it wandered all over the paper. I called out to my wife: I found I couldn't stand up. In five minutes I couldn't speak and I couldn't walk. I knew that I had had a cerebral hemorrhage, a stroke. It might well have been fatal. I was helpless, and in a few minutes reduced to a childhood condition.

Spiritually, I couldn't pray or read my Bible for months. Mentally, I couldn't think, couldn't concentrate. Physically, I was weak as a child. This lasted for seven or eight months. One time, I suddenly found that the devil was hurling everything at me. I thought it just like him to take advantage of a situation like this. He began to put into my mind sinful thoughts. Temptations that I thought I'd gotten rid of for twenty years came back at me with overwhelming force, and I had no power to resist—temptations of impurity, bad language, temptations to blow my top with my wife and children. They had a father and husband who had reverted to childhood.

In the midst of all this, when I was absolutely desperate, I cried out to God and said, "Oh, God, get me out of this mess. Lord, take me on to heaven. I can't stand any more of this attack of the devil. I can't lie here like this. I don't want the last memories that my family have of me to be of a man who lived like a cabbage, helpless for all of his life. Lord, save me. Let me die right now!"

Though I had no dramatic sense of God's presence, the conviction came to my heart born of the Spirit who said to me, "You've got all this wrong. Satan hasn't got the slightest thing to do with it. This isn't from the devil. It's from me. I had to bring you to this point in order that you might understand that this is the kind of man you always will be, but for the grace of God."

I knew it in theory, but now I knew it in experience that God is not in the self-improvement business. He's in the Christ-placement business. He's always been wanting me to make room for him. Then he said to me, "Just take a look and a long think into the past thirty years."

Then I went back to the time when I started to minister in London—fourteen years over there, ten years at Moody Church in Chicago, two or three years in Edinburgh. And I saw the building up of pressures, problems, work.

Oh, I thought it was so spiritual, for I was working like any slave for the sake of God's dear Son seven days a week, fourteen hours a day, sometimes more.

There was no time for home, no time for family, no time for anything but work. I had substituted work for the Lord Jesus, service for heart surrender, orthodoxy for obedience. I was so proud of my neat sermon outlines—three points, introduction, and conclusion, all points beginning with the same letter. I had substituted my knowledge of truth for my knowledge of God.

Remember Paul's great desire—"That I might know him." Not that I might know truth. The one is important, of course, but it is only the gateway to the other—"That I may know *him*."

I saw it all, and I could do nothing but weep. I was at the end of my rope, and when I knew that, "from sinking sands he lifted me, from shades of night to plains of light. Oh, praise his name, he lifted me!"

And today I am restored.

I'm not suggesting that God is going to do that sort of thing with everyone, but I am suggesting that he insists on restored relationships. If you feel yourself sinking under burdens and pressures, don't simply preoccupy yourself with the circumstances. Turn instead to the Sovereign of the universe and cry out, as did Peter, "Lord, save me." He will. ●

When My Daughter Ran Away Anonymous

I never thought that my 16-year-old daughter would be a part of those grim statistics—one more added to the 100,000 teenagers that run away from home every year!

We're an average Christian family; we have devotions together almost every night after dinner, and we attend church and Sunday school regularly. My husband and I have not been legalistic or overly negative with our children. We've been a closely-knit family; we like to do things together. On Friday nights we look forward to a cozy family time.

It was a Friday afternoon, and we were anticipating the usual relaxing family time, when we learned our daughter was gone! My first reaction was disbelief. I must be asleep . . . guess I've read too many stories lately . . . it couldn't happen in our family . . . I'll wake up in a minute and find it is just a bad dream!

Questions tumbled over and over in my mind. Why? Where? Who should we call first? Where have I gone wrong? Is God trying to tell me something or punish me?

I remember the young police officer who came with all the confidence of those who are new in a job. "Trouble, eh? Don't worry, she'll be back before dark. This kind of thing happens every day. Autumn's a bad time for depression—lots of suicides, kids running away. Have you got a picture?" I tried to appear interested and composed as he told about his fascinating job, but my whole body was aching and my eyes stung with unshed tears.

We found a typical note in a dresser drawer—"I love you all; don't worry." The first night was agony. There was the deafening silence of the telephone and doorbell which did not ring. My daughter used to phone a couple of times an evening when she was just next door baby-sitting. We prayed—constantly—and sought help from God's

Word. The Psalmist David came closest to my feelings of loneliness and heartbreak. He was a man who was acquainted with the agony of difficulties in family relationships. I repeated with him: "O my God, I cry in the daytime, but thou hearest not; and in the night season and am not silent" (Ps. 22:2). There was no word through the long night—the porch light was left on, and sleep was fitful.

Morning always brings hope. My husband and detectives pored over endless passenger lists at the airport. There was a ray of hope as a ticket agent recognized her picture and was able to find her flight and destination—600 miles away on the New England seacoast. There were long-distance phone calls . . . more checking for hints . . . and still not a word. David seemed to be speaking again as contact after contact failed. "It is better to trust in the Lord than to put confidence in man" (Ps. 118:8).

Three days, and still no word. She might be dead. We talked about this and the plans to be made if this was so. I pictured a broken, molested body on a lonely highway—or a body being tossed against the rugged cliffs by cold, frothing waves in the area to which she had gone. It all sounded melodramatic and like a story, but we had to face reality. I tried to resign myself as I longed that she had known more of life—I felt with David as he cried: "O my son Absalom . . . would God I had died for thee . . ." (2 Sam. 18:33).

Four days—and then my husband took off for the general vicinity of her destination on a wild chance that he might find her. He was prepared to cover miles of seacoast, checking the maze of motels that were now boarded up for the season.

I will always remember the night he phoned. "I've found our daughter, would you like to speak to her?" I was nearly hysterical with joy as I heard her voice. We both cried, though separated by many miles.

God was aware of our tears. He had timed my husband's searchings so that somehow he had found her. God had protected her. There were still many unsolved problems, but God had given life and hope.

I am sorry that I cannot write a happily-ever-after ending, nor can I formulate ten easy rules on how to prevent daughters from running away. But I believe I have learned more about God's love.

I realize that God is not any more on my side than on my

daughter's. He is as close to her as he is to me. Sometimes we parents are rather presumptuous in thinking that we have more of an "in" with God and that he only speaks to our children through us. God is concerned with my teenager as an individual, and I must relinquish her to him. I may have failed many times in my relationship with her, but God can use even these mistakes. Sometimes God can deal with her through me, but sometimes not.

I learned to thank him for the gift of friendship. The understanding and sharing in sorrow of friends was very valuable. I found a kinship with those who had similar problems. As Christians we need to share more and be honest with one another. We're famous for our play-acting, you know. Some Christians act as if they have all the answers and no problems—they are not interested in listening or sharing.

I learned that the presence of God may be keenly felt and that his voice may be clearly heard. C. S. Lewis has commented: "God whispers in our pleasures, but shouts in our pains."

God's love is unconditional. Several days before my daughter ran away, she hugged me and repeated a question several times: "Would you love me no matter what I did?" Thinking that this was just teen-age dramatics, I assured her in great superlatives that I would always love her. As I have thought since of my own love for her and how it has deepened, I have realized again and again the depth of God's love. "Great is our Lord . . . his understanding is infinite" (Ps. 147:5).

I have learned, too, that we cannot be assured that just because we have done all the acceptable, traditional Christian things, that our children will turn out in the same mold as other Christian young people we know. I think sometimes that we expect them to conform to our Christian image rather than to an image which may be peculiar to them and which God may wish to perfect.

I appreciate the happy, secure times when we are all together as a family. However, I know that God is just as much with us in the times of tragedy and separation. I also know that: "The Lord will perfect that which concerneth me" (and her!) (Ps. 138:8). ●

93

Now I Have Abundant Life by Joan Blackwood

Two years ago while I was shopping in a department store one of the salesladies whom I had come to know shocked me. "Don't you ever smile?" she asked. Did I never smile? What a terrible testimony I am for the Lord! I immediately thought.

Six months ago another saleslady in a different department store, who also knew me by sight, asked, "Aren't you ever unhappy?"

Something had happened in the interval that changed me and the question.

I was saved as a teenager at a New York Billy Graham Crusade. All through high school I lived for the Lord and then happily went away to Bible school. There I met a wonderful man; we fell in love, and three years later we were married. After graduation he went into the ministry and so I became a pastor's wife.

Over the next nine years we ministered in two pastorates and I had the opportunity to serve Jesus in many different ways. During those years we were also blessed with three healthy boys. If anyone had reason to be happy, I did. But in fact I was totally miserable. You see, although there were blessings, there were also problems. And the problems had become so great my life was a burden to me.

During that wretched summer two years ago God gave me the promise in Jeremiah: "I will surely deliver thee, and thou shalt not fall by the sword, but thy life shall be for a prey [prize] unto thee; because thou hast put thy trust in me, saith the Lord" (39:18). I said to myself, "Well, thank you, Lord, for the verse, but my life will never be a prize to me."

I was wrong.

I had known the Lord for some 20 years. Many times I had rededicated my life, and at times I had had glimpses of "the promised land" of joyful living in Christ Jesus. But I had not really "entered in" to possess it.

"Is this all there is to the Christian life?" I wondered. "Will I always 'go under' when the problems come?"

I prayed for help—and things got worse! There came a day when things became so bad and I was so low that all I could do was look up to God. Let me explain.

When I gave my life to the Lord I gave him everything—or I thought I did. But I was born with a certain amount of talent, some good looks, average intelligence, and a pleasant personality. So when I gave my heart to the Lord I felt I had a lot to offer him, something he could use for the furtherance of his kingdom on earth—*me*.

That was my big mistake. Do you know why Moses did not get into the Promised Land? It was because Moses took credit that belonged to the Lord.

Over the years I had done the same thing. I thanked God for all he had given me—but I clutched some of the glory for myself. Therefore, for me also there was a wilderness wandering, with only a glimpse of my promised land now and again.

Second Corinthians 4:7 says, "We have this treasure in earthen vessels, that the excellency of the power may be of God, and not of us." For most of my Christian life, as I look back on it now, I must have felt my vessel was at least made of brass. I was surely worth something to God, and I wanted to shine, too. I wanted to hold on to the good feelings that came when I was complimented, but that part of me that felt so good when praised was also plunged into deep depression when things went wrong.

Then God took me through circumstances to the lowest point I had ever reached, and in that low place he gently whispered, "Find all your joy in me." Out of sheer desperation I obeyed. When you feel there is nothing left to be joyful about, you are willing to find your joy in the Lord.

I began to find my joy in who he is, not what he had done for me, for it seemed he had done nothing for me for a long time. As I began to worship him and praise *him* my view of the Promised Land got better.

Then God began to deal with me about my willingness to submit to his will as Scripture points it out. Ephesians 5:22 had always irked me: "Wives, submit yourselves unto your own husbands, as unto the Lord." Many times I thought I had a better idea, and if not in word I would resist my husband in attitude. God made it clear that I was to submit to my husband just as to the Lord. I began to yield, and as I did new joy came.

As I obeyed, God restored. As I obeyed, he purged. As I obeyed, he became totally precious to me.

The song goes: "Something beautiful, something good— / All my confusion—he understood; / All I had to offer him was brokenness and strife, / But he made something beautiful of my life." When we come to him for salvation all we can offer him is brokenness. And when we come to him for service, brokenness is again all we have to offer him. I offered him brokenness. He gladly took it and made it beautiful. My life is a prize to me now. I have a treasure within me—and this vessel is going to stay earthen.

The Promised Land is no longer a promise to me. It is a reality. Does that mean I have it all? Oh, no. There are giants in the land that yet need to be conquered, but I have the promise of 1 John 4:4, "Greater is he that is in you, than he that is in the world." ●

I Couldn't Start Eating by Yvonne Sybring

I stared into the mirror at the bleak, gray eyes in sunken sockets, until tears began to fill the eyes. I felt wetness on my cheeks and was shocked that the emaciated face, the tears, were really mine.

Yes, I was the scarecrow figure, and I was slowly killing myself by refusing to eat. I had what doctors call anorexia nervosa, an overwhelming fear of food.

I knew I was slowly starving, but I couldn't make myself eat. I covered my face, shutting out the pathetic figure in the mirror, and crumpled to my bed, sobbing hopelessly.

It didn't make sense that this could happen to *me*. At 17 I was supposed to be a model kid—with good grades, a nice home, great parents, and many friends. I should have been enjoying life, but I seemed bent on ending it all.

The seeds of my nightmare had been sown long before. Even as a little girl I'd been a dreamer, wishing I could be as beautiful as the magazine cover girls. But by the time I was 16 my dreams were making me miserable. Unlike the cover girls, I had dull hair, bad skin, and plain features. And my figure—well, it just wasn't there.

"Please change me, God," I prayed, hoping for some kind of miracle. But the miracle didn't happen. Growing more and more dissatisfied with myself, I began to blame God for my "ugliness."

That summer things got worse. Working at a resort in northern Canada for two months, I watched in despair as my weight climbed from 118 to 140 pounds. When I came home to Toronto I hated the way I looked. So did the guy I'd corresponded with and dreamed about all summer. He dropped me for another, more attractive girl.

Angry, I confronted God. I blamed him for my weight gain and cursed him for my looks. But my appearance remained unchanged. That's when I got this idea.

I'd go on a diet. Even if my face would never make the cover of *Vogue*, at least I could be slim.

It started innocently enough. After all, it was just a diet. But gradually I became obsessed with losing weight, and within months my obsession was out of control.

Summer arrived again, and I returned to the resort. But this time, instead of overeating, I exercised like a maniac and ate like a bird. By the time I came home I was little more than a walking scarecrow. In eight months I had gone from 140 to 87 pounds.

I had developed anorexia nervosa. The idea of eating, of gaining even an ounce, terrified me. Just as terrified were my parents, who frantically tried to force me to eat. At first they thought I was just being stubborn. But when no amount of scolding, threatening, pleading, or crying could persuade me to put food in my stomach, they realized something was dreadfully wrong.

They watched as their once-friendly daughter became a surly recluse. I grew sullen, irritable, fearful. My bones began to protrude. My hair fell out. My smile disintegrated with disuse. So the only emotion I felt was self-hatred. I begged God to let me die.

I'll just vanish, just fade into the air, I thought. I'd lost all hope of survival and even told myself I was ready to die. Finally I was so resigned to my impending death that I sat down and wrote out a batch of invitations—to *my own* funeral.

But they were never sent. At that point God stepped in and reminded me through my mother that life really was worth living.

"Yvonne," Mom said one day, "it's one thing for you to destroy yourself. But do you realize you are also destroying God's temple? Or had you forgotten that his Spirit lives in each Christian?"

Her words stopped me. For the first time in months I felt a twinge of hope. If God's Spirit had never left me, if he hadn't given up, then perhaps I could have a future after all.

At last I was able to admit to God that I had a problem. I told him I needed his help, and I asked his forgiveness for turning my back on him. "Please release me from this fear," I begged.

In the weeks to come, my decision to live triggered a tremendous battle. I felt as if God and Satan were fighting over my survival. And I was fighting for my life as well.

Satan had clouded my thinking so thoroughly that I lived in terror for much of the next nine months. My fear of food had been so magnified that I became sick when I ate. I seemed to hear voices telling me that I was losing control, that even a bite would make me uglier and fatter than ever.

When I managed to swallow a meal, I would be consumed by guilt.

I wanted to obey God, to take care of my body, but I was afraid. My nerves were frayed, and my mind felt as though it were being torn in two.

One summer day came a turning point. I had just made myself a perfectly delicious, nutritious lunch and had brought it into the backyard to eat.

Just as I was about to take the first bite, those accusing "voices" began to scream inside my head.

"You don't need that!" they shouted. "You're just a big, fat pig!"

My heartbeat quickened. *Yes, yes, you're right*, I thought. *I'm losing control. I'm nothing but a slob.*

Perspiring, I stood up and looked around wildly, searching for a place to bury my food. I'd carefully prepared the meal, and my body needed it desperately—but all I wanted to do was dig a hole in the garden to hide the food.

I would have done it too, but at that moment a Bible verse popped into my head. It wasn't a verse I recalled memorizing, but there it was: "If the Son therefore shall make you free, ye shall be free indeed" (John 8:36). Immediately another verse came to mind: "For God hath not given us the spirit of fear; but of power, and of love, and of a sound mind" (2 Tim. 1:7). I knew God was speaking to me through both verses, and I knew what I had to do. Right there I fell to my knees and began to thank him for my food, for my freedom, for the power to eat and enjoy the meal.

For the next nine months I repeated this process, depending on God's Spirit to give me the power to eat. I was gradually learning to depend on him. Slowly my weight increased, and my fear of eating subsided.

It was nine long months, but when it was over God had healed me of anorexia nervosa.

Today, three years later, he has also taught me to accept myself. No longer do I rage against him for my "ugliness"—I can see some flaws, but also some good points. And I try to yield all of them to him.

After my experience with anorexia, I'll always know that God exists. After all, he fought for my survival when I was little more than a scarecrow—and won. ●

What's Up, Doctor? by John D. Jess

Can a spiritual Christian have a nervous breakdown? Many would answer this question in the negative. It is assumed that when a person trusts Jesus Christ as Savior, he takes out insurance against any sort of emotional imbalance. If that is true, a Christian who manifests any symptoms of nervousness or depression must be labeled a spiritual failure.

But do the facts substantiate that conclusion? I don't think so.

Time was when I attributed every trial—emotional or otherwise—to either a spiritual weakness or some form of divine chastisement. But no longer. Allow me to share some of the reasons for altering those conclusions.

GENETIC FACTORS

Although I am not a psychologist, I have studied enough case histories to know that childhood training and environment often bear directly on one's fears, attitudes, and emotional make-up. A sincere trust in Christ inevitably improves one's mental habits, but conversion does not insure against all emotional ills, any more than it does against physical illnesses. Many people who live ungodly lives have no emotional problems. This may be a reflection of their early training or a fortunate emotional inheritance; but in any event it is no credit to them. It does not prove that ungodliness produces stability nor that commitment to Christ begets instability.

Some Christians inherit a nervous disposition from one or both of their parents. It is psychologically valid that both physical and emotional traits are often passed on through parents, just as certain physical features are. A mother who suffers deep depressions may pass on to her child these depressive tendencies. And while this is not inevitable, it is common. Consequently, many Christians must

101

contend with emotional problems all their lives due to their genetic composition.

PHYSICAL SYMPTOMS

Moreover, an emotionally disturbed or depressed Christian may be suffering from a physical maladjustment, possibly a chemical maladjustment, in the body. Modern medical science has established this beyond any reasonable doubt. I am certain there are myriad Christians who think they have a *spiritual* problem when in reality it is in the physical realm.

In recent years, for example, it has been established that hypoglycemia, a low blood-sugar condition, often causes memory lapses, temper tantrums, incoherence, depression, and even suicidal tendencies. I have had some experience with this deficiency.

Other maladies are diabetes and brain damage. I recently read of a woman who was under psychotherapeutic treatment for years before it was discovered that she had a brain tumor so advanced that she succumbed before it could be removed surgically. Yet every psychiatrist has been taught that a brain tumor can cause behavior resembling neurosis and psychosis.

It must not be assumed that Christians are immune to such physical and mental debilitations, so what may be diagnosed by a well-meaning but misdirected Christian counselor as a spiritual problem may be a physical complication affecting the mind and therefore beyond the individual's control. Such a person needs medical — possibly even surgical — help. A Christian suffering from emotional stress, including mental depression, should consider a thorough medical checkup, including a five-hour glucose test, which will determine whether a high or low blood-sugar condition exists.

PERFECTIONIST SYNDROME

Another reason some Christians face real problems in the emotional realm is because they or someone else has set too high a standard. Many will argue that a Christian cannot set too high a standard for himself, but if the standard is *perfection*—absolute sinlessness, comparable to that of Jesus Christ—then the consequence can only be bitter disappointment. And this may lead to emotional instability, self-flagellation, morbidity, and a feeling of abject failure.

God wills that we do not sin, and avoidance of sin should be the goal of every Christian. But John, writing to Christians, says, "If we say that we have no sin, we deceive ourselves, and the truth is not in us" (1 John 1:8). And he spells out the provision God has made for sinning Christians: "If we confess our sins, he is faithful and just to forgive us our sins, and to cleanse us from all unrighteousness" (1 John 1:9).

REAL GUILT FEELINGS

I have not yet mentioned a very important reason why some Christians are unhappy, depressed, emotionally disordered, and, for all practical purposes, useless to God. That reason is deliberate, persistent sin against the will of God. Spiritual therapy and healing are required in this case.

The Christian who sincerely lives his faith, learns complete trust, and guards his attitudes will invariably be a healthier person. Even when there are physical factors which make it difficult to stay on the track emotionally, the Spirit-led abandonment of such faults as self-pity and resentment over one's "lot in life" can establish a deeper, more serene relationship with Christ. This will help to settle a multitude of problems which could threaten his well-being.

I caution Christians to avoid hasty judgments of those who have suffered a nervous collapse. Better would it be to say, "There, but for the grace of God, go I," than to arbitrarily attribute their condition to weak spiritual footing.

There is little doubt that faith, when properly applied, will hasten recovery from a nervous breakdown. Many psychologists and psychiatrists acknowledge that nothing is more helpful in recovering from a psychotic condition than a buoyant trust in the goodness of God and in his power to heal mentally and physically.

Sometimes unpleasant experiences are the ones which bring us closest to God. My experiences with him are not always exhilarating; sometimes they are very painful! But it is thrilling to know that all such experiences may teach us to trust him in a new, beneficial, and permanent way! ●

Saved from
Suicide Anonymous

$\mathbf{A}$ full moon guided my steps as I walked rapidly over familiar streets. There was no thought of the danger to a woman of 25 alone on the streets of a large Ohio city. I saw nothing but the way before me, heard nothing but my own tormenting thoughts, felt nothing but the misery of my life as I made my way to the bank of the river. One thought possessed me above all others—I must end it all!

My pace slowed as I drew near the water. It looked forbidding, though still inviting me to what I thought would be rest. Suddenly a fear of death took hold of me, and I came to an abrupt stop. On a large stone, I sat down, weeping.

What was I to do? I couldn't bear to go on living, but I was afraid to die.

My brain pieced together the torn fragments of my life that had led me to the wretchedness in which I found myself . . .

My father was a prominent businessman in a large Midwestern city—too busy for his family. We had social standing, were active Christian Science Church members, but, oh, so lacking in love. I was a sickly child and fearful that death would take my mother from me.

Craving love I did not have at home, I buried myself in the fine arts as a teenager. Then came the dreaded day and hour—my mother died.

Where did she go? What happened after death? Would I see her again, ever? Did death end all?

I stood numbly by her casket with these questions racing through my mind. All my security was gone. How was I to face the future? Who was there to care? With my delicate constitution, how was I to face this hard world alone? My father was too busy to notice my needs, and he expected me to face life on my own on completion of college. He said my sickness was only imaginary.

A deep bitterness against God took hold of me. I left my mother's funeral service convinced that the only service religion gave mankind was a drug to soothe troubled consciences and a tool to gain personal ends.

A sophomore in college, I tried to bury my sorrow in studies. One of my classmates tried to help me to turn to God. But I had had enough of the hypocrisy of religion. "If there is a God, it is impossible to know Him!" I declared.

Then a wild hope rose: my French professor—twice my age — showed a romantic interest in me. At last, someone to love and cling to! I was madly in love. We went away together for a week, and then when we returned, the professor threw me over!

I was desperate, and then overcome with guilt. I thought for the first time of taking my life, but fear kept me back.

Twenty-one years of age, and tormented by guilt. Would any decent man want me? I felt tired and old; life was mechanical and hopeless. I continued working on my college degree only because Dad expected me to finish college.

It was wartime, late 1941, and I met a young navy flier—a nice young man with high ideals. It was love at first sight—the right kind of love. With the future so dark, we decided to postpone marriage until the war was over.

He went overseas in 1942. It was my last year of college, and I lived for the arrival of each letter from him. At Christmas 1943, he wrote, "Darling, I expect to be back in the States in six months. We won't wait until the war is over. We'll get married then."

On Jan. 4, 1944, a telegram arrived: "Missing." I had to wait 18 days for more news: his body was found on a mountainside . . . foggy weather . . . the plane crashed . . .

My nerves were shattered. I found I couldn't sleep without phenobarbital. Nowhere could I find release from my sorrow, the guilt of the past, or the emptiness of the present.

Then I made a discovery. Becoming a little intoxicated gave a soothing sense of release. It made me forget. I plunged into a gay life of drinking and men. Live it up! Tomorrow we may die! So what? Who cared whether I lived or died? Certainly not my sophisticated companions.

The release through alcohol was only temporary. It gradually became a necessary part of my life. My sense of guilt increased, requiring more liquor to drown it.

I saw my life going down, down, tobogganing on the road to ruin. Whenever I saw a poor wretch of a woman, I would ask myself, "What is to stop me from getting like that?" I knew I couldn't stop myself. Yet I was not going to end up like those wrecks of womanhood. I would kill myself first . . .

Yes, there was no other way. I rose from the stone at the water's edge and moved toward the river. No longer weeping, only cold and unfeeling.

Suddenly, something arrested my attention. On the other side of the river stood a large, luxuriant tree sharply silhouetted in the moonlight. Its stark beauty gripped me, and the words of Joyce Kilmer's poem "Trees" began to run through my mind, ending with: "Only God can make a tree."

"Yes," I said to myself, "that tree didn't just happen. Only God could make a tree like that—only God . . ."

I looked down at the palm of my hand, the lines clearly visible in the moonlight. "I didn't come from a monkey," I exclaimed. "God made that hand. Yes, and God made me!"

I looked up into the sky and cried out from the depths of my heart, "O God, I believe You exist. I believe You made this world and universe, that tree. I believe You made me. I've made such a mess of my life. I can't straighten it out. I'm asking You to do it."

A profound sense of peace came over me. I turned and returned to my boardinghouse room and a restful sleep.

I didn't find God right away, but a hunger to know Him and lead a good life grew in my heart. Soon I moved to an eastern city, and there I met a girl who told me about Christ. I began reading the New Testament, and at my friend's suggestion I tuned my radio to Charles Fuller's "Old-Fashioned Revival Hour."

As I listened to Dr. Fuller, I came under deep conviction of sin. I struggled against it, however, wondering if God could possibly deliver me from my love of whisky.

Finally, a week before my 28th birthday as I listened to Dr. Fuller, I called on God to save me and I committed my all to Jesus Christ. It was a wonderful experience. My deliverance from whisky was immediate, and I knew the power of God in my life.

I attended Bible school, and today I work in the office of a Christian organization. I enjoy witnessing with tracts personally.

The Lord has not seen fit to restore me to good health, and I have had much physical suffering, but I have found His grace sufficient! I have also had spiritual ups and downs as I failed to draw upon "His exceeding great and precious promises." But I know the reality of Jeremiah 15:16, "Thy Word was unto me the joy and rejoicing of mine heart." Truly in God I have found all the love and security I needed for life, and for eternity. ●

Children Ask About Death by LaVernae J. Dick

I shall never forget the sound of seven-year-old Tom's feet as he raced across our wooden porch shortly after I came home from the funeral of a close friend. He jerked open the door and stuck his head in far enough to ask, "How did she look, Mom?"

It climaxed the many questions he had asked me and comments he made about death while he was becoming aware that death as well as birth is something we all share in. One day he came running into the kitchen where I was ironing to ask me, "When are you going to die, Mom?"

Another day, after I had come home from a long day at the hospital when his father had surgery, he asked, "Well, is he dead yet?" Then there was that day when he and I were listening to the news about the assassination of President Kennedy and he threw himself across his bed, announcing, "If he is dead, then I want to die, too."

Every child asks questions about death. Perhaps he does not ask them in the way Tommy does, but he asks them and deserves an answer. Even an adult knows that it is not easy to think about death. None of us can visualize our own death. Yet when we are forced to think about it we are reminded that our body will die.

Not answering a question a child asks about death does not put it out of his mind. Kathleen, aged three, was not told of the sudden death of her grandma who lived nearby. Her parents decided that she was too young to understand, and the best way to avoid talking about it was never to mention Grandma again.

Because her parents did not talk about Grandma, any questions that Kathleen asked about her went unanswered. Soon Kathleen never mentioned her either. But that did not mean that she had forgotten. Several months later when Grandpa was expected for dinner, Kathleen saw him and a lady come driving up the long driveway. As soon as the car stopped in the yard, she rushed out the door, screaming, "Oh, Grandma, you've come back!"

Then she saw the face of the woman and realized that it wasn't her grandma after all. Coming back into the house, she sobbed, "Mommy, I'm sick."

Kathleen learned about the reality of death in a very harsh way and this pitiful experience could have been avoided. Talking about death does provide a better way. Someplace between the ages of five and seven, a child begins to realize that life ends and most children ask some questions about it. What kind of answers should parents give? How can you guide your child into a meaningful understanding of death?

By all means, don't wait until a death comes to the family before you begin to discuss death. "Dear God," wrote Mike in the book, *Children's Letters to God*, compiled by Eric Marshall and Stuart Hample, "what is it like to die? Nobody tells me. I just want to know. I don't want to do it."

Things around us die all the time. In the fall plants are killed by the frost, but in the spring, plants come alive. By pointing out this normal cycle, the reality of death comes to a child in a calm, natural way. He learns that when one phase of life is over, it does not end. From seeing the reality of this process and knowing what has happened in plant life, he can by faith easier accept the fact that the death of a human being is not the last sleep, but the last final awakening. It is only his body which has died and become useless. The person continues to live with God where he continues to love those whom he loved before.

Dr. C. Everett Koop, surgeon-in-chief at the Children's Hospital in Philadelphia, feels that children who ask questions about death are old enough to assimilate knowledge about the subject.

One bright summer day, Tommy asked, "When are you going to die, Mom?" The question was really his own way of asking, "Am I going to die?" He was beginning to realize that death would be a part of his life also.

A young boy who was dying asked his mother what would happen when he died. She said to him, "Remember, when you were small, you used to go to sleep in our bed. Then in the morning when you would wake up, you'd be in yours?"

"Yes," he said, "I remember."

"Who carried you to your own bed?"

"Daddy did."

"Well, when you die, even though you cannot picture it now, just as you cannot remember Daddy carrying you to your own bed, God will carry you to His home in heaven."

In the past, sometimes parents have said too much about being ready to meet God. So much, in fact, that some children have feared death because they felt any wrong-doing, no matter how small, would send them to hell. If it is true that God knows our frame is dust and understands our failures, then He wants us to know the facts about death and what He expects of our lives on earth. But we need not continually dwell on the fact of being prepared.

Neither is it natural to want to die. Undoubtedly the Apostle Paul speaks of death in such glowing terms because of the circumstances he found himself in. We are earthbound and earth-oriented. God gave us the desire to live on earth and find joy and happiness here. It is when life becomes unbearable because of pain or circumstances that we begin to think about the joy of being in heaven and desire to be there.

If we want our child to understand a loving God, then it would seem better not to dwell only upon the fact that God calls people to Himself and heaven from this earth, through death. It is also important to help him realize the frailty and weakness of humanity. He should know that mistakes, poor judgment, lack of sufficient scientific knowledge, the need for better preventive measures, and war take people in death from us.

Mark went with his daddy who is a doctor to visit Aunt Aggie who had a form of terminal cancer. "You know, Mark," his daddy said on the way home, "Aunt Aggie has a disease and she is going to die."

"I don't want her to die," Mark protested. "I like her very much."

Several days later when Mark went with his father again to visit Aunt Aggie, she said to him, "I have so much pain, Mark. I would like to go to heaven soon."

As Mark was saying his bedtime prayers that evening, he prayed, "You can take Aunt Aggie home to heaven now so she won't hurt any more."

Mark had begun to realize that there is a time to die as well as a time to live.

When Grandpa Bob passed away, Daddy sat down with his four young children to talk about it. "You know," he said, "that part of Grandpa which talked to you, listened to what you said, saw what you did, has gone to live with God. So when we go to the mortuary all we will see is his body which will not know that we are there because that part of him which thinks is gone to be with God."

He talked about other thoughts Christians believe about death. People shall know each other in heaven and when people who know each other die, they shall enjoy their company in heaven. A person is active in heaven without pain or handicaps. Life is good and without trouble in heaven. And people there shall never leave the presence of God who is a loving and kind Father.

Later that day Tommy's family went for a drive in the country. Tommy was still thinking about Grandpa as he saw the white, fleecy clouds roll by. He remembered that heaven, God's home and where the part of Grandpa that thinks and knows is, was far above the clouds. Then he said, "Daddy, I think Grandpa is very happy now because he is with his mother and daddy and he hasn't seen them for a long time."

"Yes," Daddy replied as he smiled. "I think heaven is a happy place."

"But, Daddy," Tommy said, later, "if the part of Grandpa which thinks is gone to heaven, why do we have a funeral?"

For most Christians, the purpose of a funeral is to give help and strength for those left behind. Dr. Edgar N. Jackson says the ceremony gives people an opportunity to act out their deep emotional feelings.

Death is a fact of life. Fear of it springs from ignorance. As parents we help our children make preparations for life. Why not help them to understand, as Johnson says, that "it is impossible that anything so natural, so necessary, and so universal as death, should ever have been designed by God as an evil to mankind"? It first begins by being honest in answering the questions they ask about it. ●

111

Warn
Them of the
Wolves by Sally Wilson

Our quiet Texas town was jolted one warm September afternoon when the local radio announced that a teenager was missing from a hamburger drive-in. She was to meet her mother at 2 P.M., but she wasn't there. Circumstances led her parents and police to suspect the worst—kidnapping. Her parents' deepest fears were realized when her body was found ten days later in a gravel pit about 40 miles away. No suspect was ever captured.

Tragedy struck again a few months later when a high school junior was raped and killed after she had car trouble at night.

I began to wonder if these two girls could have prevented the situations which led to their tragedies. Then turning to my own situation, I quizzed myself: *What should I be teaching my son and daughter as they grow up about personal safety to help them avoid dangerous situations?*

Checking with our local police department, I discovered a wealth of information which they are anxious to share with the public through programs and pamphlets. Crime prevention specialists believe that most crimes, including assault crimes, are the combination of desire and opportunity. The victim unknowingly presents the right set of circumstances for a person to do harm. While it's doubtful that we can curb criminal desire, we can teach our children to avoid presenting the opportunity for assault.

Without creating unreasonable fears and suspicions, we can teach our children commonsense rules so they won't be easy targets for dangerous persons. The following safety ideas, developed by police crime prevention units and the National Child Safety Council, are arranged by age groupings for new experiences a child has as he grows up.

Young Children — Ages 5 Through 8

"Tommy is so friendly, he'd get in the car and go with anybody." Have you ever said that about your child? I have. I am pleased that my son is sociable. It's part of the wonderful naivete of his preschool years. But he's five now, and it's time to start cautioning him about whom to trust.

At this age, children are beginning to break the close ties to mom and dad. They're allowed to walk alone to school, to the bus stop, or to a friend's house, or to play in the yard or park without a parent tagging along. You and your child should discuss safety ideas for the times when he's out on his own.

Together you can establish a basic pattern for a safe path to and from the school and a reasonable time when he should be expected to arrive home after school. It's best if he can walk with a friend.

Most important, you should talk about what to do when a stranger approaches.

An early lesson is never to accept gifts, money, or rides from strangers. *"If you don't know, don't go"* is a good motto. One of my neighbors even drew up a limited list of people OK'd for their child to ride with: a neighbor, the car pool, Jimmy's mom or dad, and so forth. Others not on the list are to be refused.

You might discuss the following scenario with your child.

Question: If a stranger comes to school saying that mother sent him to pick up the child, what should you do?

Answer: Report it to the principal or the teacher and ask him to check it out.

Children should be cautioned never to permit an adult stranger to join in their play. Also warn your child about playing alone in alleys, near vacant buildings, or around public rest rooms. In fact, it is a good idea to accompany your child to the rest room when out in public at a restaurant, a ball game, and so forth.

Older Children — Ages 9 Through 12

Sometime during this age period, parents begin to allow the child to be home alone. These children should be tutored on how to answer the door and the telephone when a stranger calls.

For example, you might tell your child that if he doesn't recognize

113

a visitor, don't open the door. Instead, he could call through the door or crack open a nearby window to tell the stranger his parents will be home "later." Answer any questions with: "I'm sorry, I can't say."

When answering the telephone, the child could say, "My mother isn't here now, but I'll give her your message."

Children of this age will probably enjoy playing junior detective. They can practice memorizing a stranger's appearance or the model, color, and license number of a strange car. Developing this awareness of his surroundings and the people near him might prove vital someday if he should ever have to give a description to police.

You should reinforce the idea that police, teachers, bus drivers, and other known adults are friends that your child may turn to for help.

Unfortunately, a sex molester is not always a stranger. He may be an acquaintance or even a family member, so warnings about such actions are also necessary. For example, tell your child not to allow *anybody* to touch the private parts of his body, but encourage the child to come to you if it happens.

Teenagers
As they grow toward adulthood, teenagers assume more and more independence. Hand in hand with this goes responsibility for their protection. Situations encountered by teenagers include outings far from home, baby-sitting alone at night, and driving or riding with a friend.

Stress to your teenager the importance of safety in numbers, avoiding groups with drugs, traveling in well-lighted areas, locking car doors, and checking the back seat before getting in the car. Suggest that at night it's a good idea to have keys in hand ready to unlock the door and start the car.

Instruct your teenage daughter that if the car should break down while she is driving alone, to raise the hood, then get back inside, lock all doors, roll up windows, and turn on emergency flashers. When someone stops to help, lower the window only far enough to ask the stranger to call the police, service station, or family.

Parents should stress the dangers of hitchhiking and picking up hitchhikers. The statistics are ominous for both the driver and the rider. A free ride might be the last ride.

114

If your daughter takes baby-sitting jobs, review what to do if a stranger phones or knocks at the door when she's on the job.

Helping our children grow safely to adulthood is a big responsibility. We can get help from most police departments, which are happy to present safety programs for schools, clubs, scout troops, and so forth, geared to the children's age level. Some schools are introducing a crime prevention unit into their regular curriculum. But parents remain the primary teachers of their children's safety habits. ●

Yes, I Need a Psychiatrist! by Joan L. Jacobs

Though I am a pastor's wife, God is presently revealing his love for me in the office of a Christian clinical psychologist. It is only a transition time in my life, but the experience of relief and growing calm is so real that I must share the discovery.

I write in the consciousness of the many other spiritual and physical blessings God has given me. My marriage, my children, my husband's job, our home are all part of God's goodness. God is working in our church in fresh and fruitful ways. And I know full well that if I were a wife who had just felt the last embrace of a Christian husband taken from his home to execution, my problems would melt in the intense heat of that fiery emotional trial. But we Western Christians are subject to a different kind of trial—to the many faces of depression, to shadowy goals that defy attainment, to our general preoccupation with grasping at spiritual formulas to find fulfillment. How do we meet these trials?

Twice recently I've heard someone say, "You don't need a psychologist when you have the Bible." I disagree. It may even be that reading the Bible shows a person his need for professional care. In verse after verse we are confronted with God's standard, the awesome fact that we "should be holy and blameless before him." How do we move forward to *that* standard? Some of us find ourselves facing problems that block our growth in spite of prayer, Bible study, worship, and fellowship.

Satan has ways of insinuating himself into the lives of Christians to rob them of Jesus' gift of peace and joy. Of course, multitudes of committed Christians have overcome in the light of God's Word and the strength of his presence. But at the moment my concern is with the others who are committed to Jesus Christ but for whom the battle is a despairing conflict with an unknown enemy. Often

116

for these Christians the message of the Bible, its beautiful insistence on the love of God, falls on deaf ears.

Many of the Christian psychiatrist's and psychologist's clients are troubled Christians to whom the gospel has become "bad news." They face the opportunity to work with God to "untie things that are now knotted together and tie up things that are still dangling loose" (C. S. Lewis's description of our predicament). We do Christian psychologists an injustice to call them by the term "shrink," or "head-shrinker"; for me the psychologist has been a welcome "head-spreader."

Several years ago Dr. Donald Tweedie, a professor at the graduate School of Psychology at Fuller Seminary, suggested that professional care is in order when a problem is so persistent that one has been unable to overcome it with sustained effort. He gave an example of a man who has determined to give his wife and family the personal attention and concern he knows God wants him to give but who finds that he just cannot produce anything but negative responses.

In my case the immediate problem was my inability to function compatibly with my husband in handling our children. As my husband's patience grew thin, in God's own time and way we located the right psychologist. There I found a freedom to air the problem in the presence of a skilled, accepting person.

Even as this happened, a whole thicket of brambles revealed itself—alien roots in the soil of a heart essentially bent toward God. Among the thorns was a self-consciousness that dogged me in almost every relationship, including an inability to look non-Christians in the eye and witness lovingly and without embarrassment and confusion. Too, I had begun to experience a depression, a kind of paralysis in daily living.

The handles of my problems were not hard to grasp. Together we found that I had unconsciously raised such high standards for myself and those I love most that I consciously majored in weaknesses. This led to nagging and preaching and that insidious kind of appreciation that responds only to good performance. Unnecessary feelings of guilt were there, too—not just a healthy sensitivity to sin, but self-imposed burdens. I had applied the old theologically sound "fact, faith, feeling" formula to my personal walk with Jesus and then ruled out feelings. I needed a warm, emotional experience

117

with him that would be far better than my panic-prayers and the sporadic sense of his presence. As the kinks straighten, I find my experience with God renewed. I've discovered how much he really loves me.

No one would hesitate to make distinctions between effective and ineffective ministers, but we easily lump all psychologists together. That is a mistake. There are psychologists under the name Christian whose credentials are not trustworthy, or whose personal integrity or doctrinal stand is disappointing. Many a pastor and Christian physician have been discouraged by referring a person to one of these. There are dedicated non-Christian psychologists who can provide significant help along the road to emotional health but who cannot help to smooth the path to *spiritual* maturity. And then there are some with adequate training whose chief desire is to serve God and help people, and who sensitively seek to bring it all under the limits and freedoms of their personal experience of Jesus Christ. But there are too few of these, so there are many among us in the body of Christ who need but may never have an opportunity to share my rich experience of answers found in a professional setting.

I see risks in therapy that lie in the introspection—the keen involvement with feelings—that accompany it. One can almost create another world, where the reality is the counselor's hour and much of the rest of the week is filled with thoughts about past or future sessions. Often when problems are deep, progress may not be observable. Problems that have taken a long time to come can take a long time to go. Depression may increase for a while. The client does not always leave the therapy session with a sense of well-being.

There is the additional risk of what the psychologists call "transference," when this accepting listener, who with great sensitivity allows us to see ourselves, begins to fill a role that at best can be only temporary and at worst can rob us of the health we are seeking. The good counselor maintains the balance between being involved and being impersonal. These risks have been involved in my time with the counselor. Because of the scarcity of capable therapists and often because of lack of funds, there are members of the body who need other help. I want my brothers and sisters in Christ who are hurting to be able to experience this same atmosphere of freedom and acceptance, to breathe the sweet air that is free of judgment and criticism. What would God have us do?

118

A good start is to imitate the love of Jesus, the love that led him to die for us while we were yet unfriendly, cold, critical, sour, and full of pride. What about the man who approaches you on your way into the sanctuary? Could you love him more if he spoke a little less effusively, if he were a few shades lighter, or if you could only forget the rumor that he stepped out on his wife? What about that woman toward whom you are being ushered in the pew? Could you love her more if she sang a little less enthusiastically, or if her wig were a little less obvious?

And those you love the most—are they free in your presence to be who they really are? Are they free to share without inviting a sermonette? Are friends free to cry in your presence with their frustration or heartbreak? Do you choke back pat answers in the face of tragedy and enter the struggle with quiet compassion? Or are you afraid even to be in the presence of someone who is deeply troubled? Are you open to love strangers and to break your own comfortable molds in order to accommodate them?

Sometimes Christians forget that God has the answers and that the psychologist is one of the different members of the body whom God uses. I am deeply thankful for a husband who seeks God's best for me. I am grateful for answers from my own family and from a few close friends in the larger family of God. As the Holy Spirit moves us toward one another, with our various gifts, we fulfill one another so that Jesus can be seen. And when he is not allowed to do his fulfilling work for lack of open channels, I am grateful for the work of his skilled servant, the ministering psychologist. ●

Divorce Was Not the Answer Anonymous

I stood in the sun-drenched white-and-gold bedroom with the evidence of my husband's unfaithfulness clutched in my hand. He had been incredibly careless to leave the note in a pocket of his suit. How many stories I had read of women in this predicament, never dreaming that I would one day be one of them!

Slowly I unclenched my fingers and let the paper drop. I felt immeasurably cheapened. How could a decent man do this to his wife? Images, questions, emotions, stampeded through my mind. What was the "other woman" like? How long had the relationship existed? How could it exist, and I not sense a difference in my husband of nine years?

But over and above the shock, what bothered me most was that thing crouching in the back of my mind—relief! Relief that my husband had broken his vows. It drove me to my knees, where I could only moan, "O God, help me!"

My marriage had been empty for several years. Even when I had realized, however, that it could never be built into a satisfying relationship, I saw no way out. There were Joan and Tommy to consider. Divorce was not for me. I was a Christian and must live with my mistake. Peter's infidelity now put a different face on the matter.

Strange, I had never thought of his being discontented, needing more than I was giving him. I was satisfied that the tremendous effort I was making to fulfill my obligations as his wife had deceived him.

He was so glad to get me nine years ago, my hurt pride said. Yes, he would have taken me on any terms. His ardor had swept me off my feet. Peter, a divorcé, had been a knowledgeable lover, and I had been a ready prey for this tall, attractive male. In spite of the head shakings of my Christian parents we were married and were very happy at first.

120

When had our happiness begun to fray at the edges? Peter would say I had caused a rift by getting "too religious." It was at the time of Joan's birth that I felt a strange yearning. If I were to be a fit mother for the little life entrusted to us, I would need God's wisdom. I wanted my child to have the security I had known, growing up in a godly home. So I sought out a church.

This didn't suit my worldly husband. He had not married a pious person, and thought I was cheating to make this about-face.

Looking back, it seemed to me that I had handled the situation reasonably well, however. I'd been careful never to make an issue of nonessentials and had accommodated to Peter's way of life more than I wanted to.

It wasn't until Tommy's arrival that I really fell "out of love." My husband was jealous of the baby. When it didn't wear off as Tommy grew out of infancy, Peter's immaturity disgusted me. I saw, when I began to look, how immature my husband was in almost every area. He was a sensual being with no interests, I told myself, apart from food, clothes, and shelter. He read nothing but the newspaper, and made snap judgments on every issue. His comment on the Vietnam war: They ought to drop the H-bomb and finish the job. His reaction to civil-rights problems: The Negroes should be shipped back to Africa. He made a handsome income, but he and I had nothing to talk about. He refused to share in my spiritual life, and he had no cultural appreciation of any kind.

What happened between us from the time of my disillusionment to the moment when I sat in the bedroom clutching the other woman's note? I had tried hard to cope with Peter's weaknesses. When I was overcome by the emptiness of my marriage, I would tell myself grimly, "You're fortunate—a lovely home, beautiful children, a decent man. Think of the women who are married to alcoholics or to men who run around."

But now divorce was inevitable. My mind ran in circles all day, and I was no more certain how to broach the matter to my husband when he came in at night than I had been that morning. We got through dinner, and wore away the hours until bedtime, when Peter wandered out to the kitchen for a snack. He had the refrigerator door open when I spoke. "Peter, I know about you. I know—everything."

He turned, with the milk carton in his hand. He had loosened his tie, and it was askew. He put the carton down carefully on the counter and closed the door. He gave me one look. His shoulders sagged a little as he walked over to the table and sat down. "How'd you . . .?"

"That letter, in your brown suit."

"Oh! . . . What are you going to do?"

"I wish I knew," I said wearily. I sank into a chair. "Peter, why?"

He ran a finger around his collar and shook his head. "What's the use? I couldn't ever explain." He shook his head, as if to shake a fog out of his mind. "I swear it's over as of this minute. I never really cared two cents for her."

"But, Peter! Then why?"

He hunched a shoulder. "I'm not smart with words like you. But a man's got to be more than a meal ticket in his house." His eyes followed me anxiously as I went over to the window. "I guess you couldn't forgive a thing like that; you're too good a woman."

The fact that these words didn't even prick me should have revealed my spiritual condition to me. But I merely replied numbly, "I need time to think."

As the days passed and Peter and I went through our empty routine to deceive the children, I probed to understand where I had failed my husband. I was astonished to learn that imperceptive Peter had been acutely conscious of my withdrawal and, humiliated, had sought a close relationship elsewhere.

So my well-meant pretenses had been a failure, and there was nothing left. I had an acquaintance who guessed our problem, and urged me to leave Peter. "To thine own self be true," quoted this divorcée. "Children are worse off in an unhappy home than with just one parent. Don't live a lie."

When I finally made an appointment with a lawyer, Peter was morose but did not try to prevent me. "I love you, but I want a real marriage, not a fake."

It was then, before I saw the lawyer, that Dwight Hervey Small's book, *Design for Christian Marriage*, fell into my hands. As I read this revealing study, God turned his searchlight on my life. The self-examination humbled me, a quality in which I had been singularly lacking. Only when we see our own deficiencies are we ready to accept the imperfections of others.

I had set myself up as superior to Peter. I had labeled him gross, lacking capacity for fineness, inferior in intellect. Such an attitude toward a fellow creature builds walls, and is infinitely displeasing to our Maker. I asked God to trample my pride underfoot. I prayed that I might be able to accept Peter for what he was. Jesus brought out the best there was in a man, but he did not expect more from him than he was capable of.

Could I forgive the knife-thrust to our intimacy of which my husband had been guilty? Only in Christ, for it was humbling beyond measure, and I was not a humble person.

But I saw that it would take humility on Peter's part to be forgiven, and here we could meet. As Small says in *Design for Christian Marriage*, "There is really no more wonderful way for human love to deepen than through the constant interaction of pity and forgiveness. This is the interaction of that 'secret sympathy' that binds two lovers in the bond that God intended. . . ."

I had badly failed my husband in my retreat from a close personal relationship. I had gone through all the motions, but I hadn't been there. Such proud withdrawals strike at the very heart of a marriage.

I had not understood, either, that there is incompatibility in every marriage, for no human being is without self-love. And when two self-centered beings join their lives, there is bound to be struggle, until they learn the painful lesson of loving another more than self. Peter's disillusionment, when I was faking it rather than striving toward a mature and responsible love, had driven him to another. At the same time, I saw that he would not have been so badly hurt if he had not truly loved me. With his deepening understanding we were able to talk to each other, and finally to pick up the pieces.

No good marriage just happens. We rebuilt ours, one faltering step after another, first upon a commitment to God and an acceptance of his will. Peter agreed, fearfully, to try this. Then our covenant with each other to share our lives in mutual trust and respect led us back to love, a love enriched this time by a right relationship to Christ.

Peter and I are happy together. When you look at another human being as God sees him, you feel the sympathy and concern that comes from God. His love can flood your being and flow freely toward the one with whom your life is linked. Peter will never be

123

deeply interested in many of the things I appreciate—music, literature, art—but that is one of the things I have accepted. He in turn is able to accept my deficiencies, since we are bound together by our ties to Jesus Christ. This forms the basic intimacy which permits us to be individualistic in many areas, and yet united.

Marriage reveals all the depths—and shallows—of the soul. Where love is mature there will be understanding, compassion, pity perhaps, forgiveness always. Conversely, the immature person who enters marriage with a head full of romantic dreams is quickly disillusioned. He is unable to cope with the weaknesses exposed in his partner, and those that show up unexpectedly in himself.

I would say to young people who are carried into marriage on the wave of physical attraction that the only way to avoid shipwreck is to experience an intimate relationship with God. We never live our lives in the right perspective until we regain the fellowship with him which we lost in the Fall. Once we have, we can bring our best to a marriage, for two redeemed personalities are ready for a mature relationship which will deepen and grow richer throughout life. ●

It's a Funny Thing by Carol Kivo

Magazines devote columns to it every month. The psychologists tell us it is an essential ingredient for good mental health. It isn't fattening or sinful and yet it feels good. What is this universal remedy that deserves so much of our attention? It is none other than laughter.

Laughter serves many uses. It can encourage the melting together of an audience as they listen to a speaker who uses humor well. It can soften a blow to the ego as a friend laughs with you and tells you of his goof-up, too. It can lighten a heavy burden and shorten a long day.

In my home as a child it was mostly my mother who laughed. In fact, she giggled as well. As we finished dinner some evenings, usually when my father was at work, my mother would ask, "Do you remember when . . . ?" and we each took turns relating memories until our sides ached and our eyes teared.

We giggled about how silly certain family members looked caught on the lake in a sudden rain storm. We roared about the look of anguish on my dad's face whenever my younger brother beat him handily at a game. We learned a lot about child-world events and adult-world events during our laughing sessions.

Today I treasure the ability and willingness to laugh. With children of my own, there doesn't seem to be much difficulty finding something to chuckle over. When my son was learning to walk (and fall), I said "Boom" with a lot of gusto when he landed hard. This delighted him, and he would laugh until the moment of hurt had passed. "Boom" became our private game and served us well at other times when he was sick and the whole world looked glum.

When my daughter began learning to talk, I took various nursery rhymes and turned them into little games with surprise endings.

125

My daughter soon became her own innovator and ended most games by tickling Mommy and watching Mom buckle over with the tickles.

Now that my children are older, our sessions of silliness have become more sophisticated. Last week my son asked, "Do you remember when . . . ?" and we were off giggling and snorting. When we put ourselves back together, I thought back to my childhood and was glad that I had been taught the pleasure of laughter.

The sources of laughter are everywhere, not just with children. Because we are human, we do all sorts of humorous things. We twist words, misread directions, wear different-colored socks, sleep in when we shouldn't, and forget things. We slip, trip, and stumble—emotionally as well as physically. If we can but laugh with ourselves and with others, we will go a long way toward curing our ills. Laughter, the universal remedy, is delightfully powerful. ●

Now I Win When I Lose by Debi Blackstone

For as long as I can remember there has always been someone who could do things better than I could. Even the things I most loved to do or the things I thought I was pretty good at. This was especially true in sports or sports-related activities.

As a high school cheerleader I ate, drank, and slept flips, splits, and jumps. I felt most alive when I was at a basketball or football game yelling my heart out. But there was always *that girl* whose flip was a little neater than mine or whose jump was a little higher. It made me jealous.

When I arrived at the college campus I was sure I was the number one choice from among the freshman girls for the cheering squad. But I didn't even make alternate! That "failure" was a disappointment I carried around for almost two years.

It was also in my freshman year that a group of girls tried to organize a track team. Though I wasn't fast I had plenty of endurance for the mile run, I thought. But all the other girls were upperclasswomen and had been running for years. They were all faster than me. I felt self-conscious doing sprints alongside those veterans. Lucky for me, the team was never officially organized. With my feelings of inferiority I don't think I could have competed.

In my sophomore year I plucked up enough courage to go out for the tennis team. Here was a sport I truly loved. And I thought I played a pretty good game—until the first practice. There I felt like a fool—the other girls served like pros. What in the world was I doing there?

After a few practices I dropped out. "A schedule conflict," I told the coach. But I knew that I was afraid I would fail to meet my own expectations. There was a nagging uneasiness that I would be compared to an opponent and be found wanting. Rather than battling my fears, I surrendered to them.

Why have I shared this dismal story? Why have I let myself be seen through personal failures?

Because today I am not the person I have described. I am becoming more of the woman I would like to be and can be. I have left the world of my "failures" behind and am traveling into a world where I know who I am and what I can do. In the process I am making some deep realizations.

The most warming discovery is that I am a unique person—God sees me that way! Only I can be this person called Debi. And when I do something, make some kind of effort to achieve a goal, I have to do it without fear of other individuals. I must do *my* very best, not someone else's. When I have allowed fear of failure and comparison to plague me, I have been stopped before I start.

That ugly whispering in your mind . . . "You can't do that; why embarrass yourself trying?" and the fear of comparison . . . "Forget it, you're not in the same class with the other girls" ruin many opportunities.

God gave me my body to work with, to train, to enjoy. Being ashamed of what I am and what I can do is an insult to him.

I have learned that my life is a distinct melody which is to be sung or played to the Lord. There can be no other combination of notes (my attributes and talents) that will sound quite like me. My part blends in a chorus that the Lord loves to hear.

To Christians, God is a choirmaster, not a scorekeeper. Whatever *my* song is, I have to sing it as it is. The important thing is that I sing with all my heart. ●